Mariner's Compass Quilts

New Directions

by Judy Mathieson

C&T PUBLISHING

Mariner's Compass Quilts—New Directions

©1995 Judy Mathieson

FRONT COVER PHOTO:
Starfire (detail), 84" x 84", 1993,
by Judy Mathieson

TITLE PAGE PHOTO: Wind Rose, 33" x 33", by Judy Mathieson
COVER DESIGN: Bonnie Smetts Design
EDITOR: Louise Owens Townsend
TECHNICAL EDITOR: Sally Lanzarotti
DESIGN: Irene Morris, Morris Design
COMPUTER-GENERATED ILLUSTRATIONS: Jack Mathieson,
Micaela Carr and Donna Yuen
PHOTOGRAPHER: Jack Mathieson (unless otherwise noted)

Published by C&T Publishing, P.O. Box 1456, Lafayette, California 94549

ISBN: 0-914881-97-3

Library of Congress Cataloging-in-Publication Data

Mathieson, Judy.
    Mariner's compass quilts—new directions / by Judy Mathieson
              p.   cm.
    Includes bibliographical references.
    ISBN: 0-914881-97-3
    1. Patchwork—Patterns. 2. Patchwork quilts. 3. Title.

TT835.M3767 1995
746.46—dc20   95-18374
                                        CIP

Printed in Hong Kong

10   9   8   7   6   5   4   3   2

Contents

Acknowledgments

Thanks to my husband Jack who did the photography, preliminary illustrations, and computer backup, and who gave me a sharp nudge occasionally to remind me to get to work. ✦ I appreciate the encouragement of Roberta Horton, Mary Mashuta, Marsha McCloskey, Pat Scoville, *Quilter's Newsletter Magazine*, and all the students who have helped me to learn along with them. ✦ I hope the reader enjoys the quilts of those who entrusted me with their creations or treasured antiques: ✦ Joy Baaklini, Janet Bunch, Lisa Ann Carrillo, Janet Cook, Sharon Commins, Judy Dales, Diane Leighton, Tami Marshall, Velma McCabe, Kathleen McCrady, Yoko Nomura, Fumie Ono, Marlene Peterman, Kimberly Randolph, Nancy Ryba, Eliko Sagawa, Judy Sogn, Karen Stone, and Shirley Sydow. ✦

SANTA MARIA, 82" x 82", 1992, BY VELMA McCABE, HANFORD, CALIFORNIA.

Foreword

I have been making Mariner's Compass and other circular star quilts since 1980, and it is still my favorite pattern. In 1987 I wrote the book called *Mariner's Compass: An American Quilt Classic.* The design continues to appeal to quiltmakers who seek the challenge of a dramatic design even though it requires more skill and application than other patchwork designs. I have been pleased to see quiltmakers producing exciting quilts that use my favorite stars, sometimes very traditionally and sometimes in ways that make me say, "I wish I had thought of that!"

The number of quiltmakers is increasing every year as the fabric industry produces more appealing cotton fabrics, inventive people manufacture new efficient tools, and talented quiltmakers publish exciting books on quiltmaking. I hope that this book provides some new designs and suggestions that you can add to your quilts to make them personally yours.

A wealth of books are available that cover all aspects of the quiltmaking art. I have chosen not to cover the very basic techniques since I think most people who are attracted to this pattern have skills past the beginning stage. This leaves more room for patterns.

Several recommended basic books are listed in the bibliography. If you can't locate them, ask for help at your local quilt shop and bookstores or check the public library. Quilting periodicals carry advertisements for books, and there are companies that specialize in mail ordering books of interest to quiltmakers.

▲ TWENTY-ONE POINT STAR (DETAIL), 63" x 79", CIRCA 1900, KENTUCKY. COLLECTION OF FUMIE ONO, GRANADA HILLS, CALIFORNIA.

Introduction

Piecing this design requires precision and a working knowledge of the use of templates and accurate marking, but you don't have to put it off forever just because someone told you it was difficult. I often ask my students at the beginning of a class on Mariner's Compass if they have made one before. Those who have already sewn one usually admit that it was much easier than they had envisioned. So don't let others frighten you, but do start with one that matches your skill level.

Here, in my second book on Mariner's Compass quilts, you'll find information on planning a quilt using examples from traditional to innovative. The chapter on drafting will guide you in easy steps to designing your own patterns if you wish. The section on fabric selection includes advice that I have found useful in my quilts.

There are many construction techniques available, and I have included information about traditional methods as well as freezer paper templates and paper foundations.

In Chapter Five you'll find 9 patterns for Mariner's Compass style star variations that you can mix and match as you please in your quilts. Also included is a pullout sheet that has full-size patterns for an off-center star and two different oval stars.

Mariner's Compass is the name quilters use to refer to star designs that radiate from the center of a circle as opposed to the star designs that grow from a square, like Ohio Star or Sawtooth Star. If you are going to call your quilt Mariner's Compass, the star should probably have 16 or 32 points like the compass card on a magnetic compass.

During the 16th Century, cartographers made wonderful sailing charts and let their imaginations run free. You can benefit by a study of these beautiful charts to see how the colors were used in the wind roses to indicate the principal winds and how symbols were used for the different winds. Wind roses came to be used with a lodestone to find the direction north in the magnetic compass. English-speaking countries call the emblem a compass rose. It is not clear exactly how the fleur-de-lis came to represent north on the compass rose, but it was an emblem used by the French monarchy, and many important cartographers of the time came from that country.

There are several patterns for stars inspired by these nautical style designs and some appliqué patterns for that companion design, the fleur-de-lis. While a star with a basic division of five would hardly be helpful in finding north, south, east or west, a star with any number of points or outside configuration could certainly be called a mariner's star since the stars in the night sky are also used to find direction. One of my favorite designs from my previous book, *Mariner's Compass: An American Quilt Classic*, is the 20-point Twilight Star, and I have included this pattern again but in two new sizes with a number of quilt examples.

Our own personal star, the sun, is also represented by these designs. Traditional quilt designs are sometimes called Sunburst or Sunflower, and you will find examples of these in the pattern section.

You can find design sources in almost any culture that uses these central radiating designs, and among my favorites are the painted designs on the wheels of carts from Central America, particularly Costa Rica. They often use the six primary and secondary colors in their decorations and use basic divisions of three or six.

Large star designs are perfect for the center of symmetrical medallions, and oval designs add grace to any quilt. When you get an impulse to try something a little different, begin a round design off-center to add a whole new look.

If the patterns offered here don't quite fit what you had in mind, then go to the chapter on drafting. It isn't difficult to draft your own style or size star, and once you get comfortable with the techniques, you can draft a star into any shape that suits your fancy, not just round and oval.

Quilters have been using paper templates in new ways to increase the accuracy of their results. Freezer paper, which is paper with a light plastic coating, sticks to fabric when pressed with a heated iron. It can be used for traditional designs with multiple pieces of the same pattern, but it excels in designs like the off-center stars where each pattern piece is unique and used only once. Sewing directly through paper printed with segments of the design and then tearing the paper away can also increase the control and accuracy of the finished block. You will find these new techniques, as well as the traditional methods, included here.

▲ ABOVE: A SMALL PAINTED WOODEN TOURIST SOUVENIR IN THE STYLE OF THE CARTWHEELS OF COSTA RICA. OWNED BY REV. AND MRS. L. M. MCCOY, DECATUR, GEORGIA.

Chapter One
Planning Your Quilt

What inspires a person to make a quilt? The need for bed covering, the desire to give your work as a gift, or just the pleasure of working with special fabrics are all good reasons to make a quilt. Whatever the reason that causes you to choose radiating star designs, they do have special design problems. How can I say this without sounding silly? They are so *round*, so circular and yet spiky at the same time. How do you combine them to make a quilt, which is usually some form of a square?

▲ MARINER'S COMPASS QUILT, 75" x 95", CIRCA 1870, NEW ENGLAND. COLLECTION OF NANCY RYBA, GRANADA HILLS, CALIFORNIA.

Traditional solutions for setting blocks together are a good place to start. If you place a radiating star in a block, it can have two different appearances. A star occurs if the piecing wedges that hold the circle together are the same fabric or value as the background of the square. The blocks can be set without sashing as seen in the antique quilt owned by Nancy Ryba.

▲ MARINER'S COMPASS QUILT (DETAIL).

STAR STEPS
TO HEAVEN I,
70" X 92",
1993,
BY KIMBERLY
RANDOLPH,
SHARPSBURG,
MARYLAND.
◀

You get a star in a circle if the fabrics in the background are a different fabric or value than the background in the pieced circle. Kimberly Randolph has separated her sparkly stars with pieced sashing. You can find the pattern for this star in my previous book.

VIRGINIA
SUNFLOWER
(DETAIL),
72" X 96",
CIRCA 1870,
VIRGINIA.
COLLECTION OF
THE AUTHOR.
◀

Janet Cook made *Star of David,* the champion at Quilts UK 1994, held in England. This wonderful quilt is a fabric interpretation of a mosaic pavement in London's Westminster Abbey, a masterpiece of medieval art.

▲ STAR OF DAVID, 92" x 98", 1994, BY JANET COOK, FELMERSHAM, BEDFORD, ENGLAND.

Photo by:
Kieren Flavey

Kathleen McCrady has floated stars and circles across a background of pieced fabrics that change in value and color. Her stars are almost hidden but as they emerge, they carry the theme of *In the Beginning*.

▲ IN THE BEGINNING,
80" x 62", 1991,
BY KATHLEEN H. McCRADY,
AUSTIN, TEXAS.

▲ COMPASS TO THE COSMOS,
60" x 64", 1993,
BY ERIKO SAGAWA,
YUZAWA AKITA, JAPAN.

Photo by:
Melissa Karlin Mahoney,
Quilter's Newsletter
Magazine

Japanese quiltmakers are bringing a new approach to the traditional patterns we western quiltmakers have been using. Eriko Sagawa has created a feeling of movement, and not only do her stars float, but the blocks float as well.

Judy Dales has moved her central star beyond the ordinary in *Coriolus*. Originally inspired by a design from a Costa Rican cartwheel, she removed several segments of the star and five-pointed stars fly out like candy from an exploded piñata. You will find a pattern for a similar star based on the Costa Rican cartwheel on page 80.

▲ CORIOLUS,
58" x 69", 1992,
BY JUDY B. DALES,
BOONTON TOWNSHIP,
NEW JERSEY.

Photo by:
Photo House, Inc.

Two of the stars in *Night Lights* appear to float behind the border because they are cut off. One star overlaps the border, and the rays of the three stars intersect each other's space. See page 55 for information on how to intersect star circles.

NIGHT LIGHTS, 66" x 66", 1988, BY THE AUTHOR.

▶

Joy Baaklini has a wonderful large star floating in a heavily quilted background with a serenely scalloped border. Both *Compass Rose* and *Nautical Stars* on page 36 were inspired by an ink drawing, probably by an unknown sailor, shown in Robert Bishop's book, *Folk Art Painting in America.*

COMPASS ROSE, 88" x 100", 1988, BY JOY BAAKLINI, AUSTIN, TEXAS.

◀

Photo by:
Ken Wagner

A series of tipped squares and an off-center location give Tami Marshall's *Moon Shadows* a contemporary look.

▲ MOON SHADOWS,
57" X 60", 1988,
BY TAMI MARSHALL,
ROCKFORD, WASHINGTON.

If you would like to get away from the block format, leave the stars in circles and organize them on a large square of fabric in any order you choose.

Judy Sogn has floated five large stars on a dark background in a classic symmetrical setting and surrounded them with graceful appliqué and pieced borders.

▲ WINE AND ROSES, 81" x 81", 1995, BY JUDY SOGN, SEATTLE, WASHINGTON.

Photo by: Dennis Sogn

▲ POINTS OF LIGHT, 47" x 36", 1994, BY DIANE LEIGHTON, YUBA CITY, CALIFORNIA.

▲ POINTS OF LIGHT (DETAIL).

Diane Leighton has floated a number of different-size stars in a dark background with a classic border to create a calm, composed feeling. See Construction chapter page 54 for advice on how to float the circles on a solid background.

▲ STARFIRE,
84" x 84", 1993,
BY THE AUTHOR.

Another way of looking at these stars is to divide them into quarter circles—a basic quilt shape. They can then be manipulated the way Fans or Drunkard's Path designs are handled.

The design for *Starfire,* shown here and on the cover, (pattern on page 83), was suggested by a Crazy quilt with Fans by Susan McCord in Indiana in 1895. I entered the design into a computer where it could be rotated and manipulated to give me new choices in design. The computer is a handy tool but the same kind of choices are possible with graph paper, a compass, and a photocopy machine.

Large single stars can be taken out of the traditional circle and drafted into a square to give them new energy. When you also put them off center, they can become almost frantic. *Epicenter* is a quilt, which was on the design wall of my workroom when the powerful Northridge Earthquake shook Los Angeles in January l994. We were only four miles from the epicenter, so it was a dramatic experience. As we cleaned up over the next few weeks, I took breaks to finish sewing the quilt together. Not only was I working on it during that anxiety ridden time with aftershocks happening often, but it reminded me of the quake—loud, erratic, and hard to live with. The border is a memorial to all of the fallen bricks from our chimney and walls. See page 27 for information on how to draft stars into squares.

▲ Epicenter, 73" x 73", 1994, by the author.

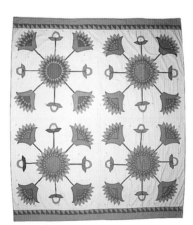

It was a memorable day when I found this *Sunflower Appliqué* quilt in an antique shop in Los Alamos, California. The central shape in each block is pieced without the pie-shaped backgrounds that form a circle and then appliquéd to the background in the middle of the classic appliqué style block. Segments of the pieced sunflower are also used in the diagonal flowers. You can find a pattern used for traditional sunflowers on page 77.

▲ Middle Left:
Sunflower Appliqué, 70" x 78",
circa 1850, unknown maker.
Collection of the author.

◄ Left: Sunflower Appliqué
(Detail).

If the blocks are stars in a circle, the background square can be composed of several fabrics, and secondary patterns will be created as seen in Janet Bunch's *Florida Doo Dah Day.*

Working with the pattern as a single large central unit is also a very classic quilt design. Tami Marshall has made a traditional style medallion with an inner border on point in *Light of the Morning.*

FLORIDA DOO DAH DAY,
72" x 72", 1993,
BY JANET M. BUNCH,
WOODBURY, CONNECTICUT.
◀

There are several other quilts in this book that display good traditional settings. *Starring Plaids* on page 62 has wonderful pieced sashing. *Plaid Mariner's Compass* has a simple sashing, but setting the blocks on point adds movement to the quilt. See page 65. *Compass Roses* is also set on point, but the sashings are appliquéd with an elegant trailing vine. See page 39.

▲ LIGHT OF THE MORNING,
92" x 92", 1989,
BY TAMI MARSHALL,
ROCKFORD, WASHINGTON.

▲ New York Beauty,
80" x 80", circa 1920, Indiana.
Collection of the author.

Karen Stone also dealt with the quarter-circle star but she was inspired to work with it by a design traditionally called *New York Beauty.* Karen made the design her own by using a variety of different points in each block and then arranging the blocks with a diagonal flow in a setting often seen in Drunkard's Path or Fan quilts. She gave it even more movement by tipping each block so that new stars were formed at each intersection. Pressed paper foundation piecing gives speed and accuracy to this kind of design, and you can find a pattern for a block similar to the antique New York Beauty, on page 72. Refer to the chapter on drafting if you would like to create a series of different designs as Karen has done.

▲ New York Beauty, 68" x 78", 1993, by Karen Stone, Dallas, Texas.

I hope you find inspiration in these pages for a quilt that could range from traditional to innovative. Consult the pattern section for the shapes that might fit your needs, or experiment with the drafting section to fill your special needs. I hope that the chapters on fabric selection and construction will help you to get your quilt onto the bed or the wall.

▲ New York Beauty (Detail).

Chapter Two
Drafting the Patterns

This book includes full-size patterns that I hope you will find useful. Also, radiating star designs are easy to draft. The traditional symmetrical stars that use a set of repeating patterns need to be drawn carefully and with as much accuracy as possible. The ones drawn full-size on paper give more flexibility and freedom, and accuracy is not as critical. If the piece fits its neighbor when you draw it and cut it apart, then it will fit when you sew it back together.

Supplies and Tools

Graph Paper. ¼" or ⅛" grid. Use the 8½" x 11" size for the 6" practice exercises; 17" x 22" is available for larger designs. Actually, plain paper is fine. I just like the grid marks to begin the squares and to use as reference marks as I go along.

18" Clear Plastic Ruler with holes. For large circles you can use a yardstick compass, available from an art supply store or quilt supply sources. Some 18" plastic rulers come with drilled holes and can be used with a sharp pencil as a compass. You can drill holes yourself in a ruler and use it to make large circles.

Sharp Pencils and Eraser. Mechanical pencils with black lead in sizes 0.5mm or 0.7mm are excellent. You will find it helpful to use colored pencils (blue, red, and green) for the first exercise to help you identify the set of lines that you are working with in each step.

Adjustable Drafting Compass. There are a variety of types available. If you are going to use one often, invest in a style that stays fixed where you set it. Some have quick release mechanisms that are handy, and some have extensions to allow them to make larger circles.

Freezer Paper. Plastic-coated paper available from grocery stores in rolls of various widths. It is also available in sheets with a ¼" printed grid from quilt supply sources.

Protractor. Available at art or drafting supply stores, this instrument helps to lay down and measure angles. Use either the 180° (half circle) or 360° (full circle) size. The accuracy of the angles will be increased if the protractor is large.

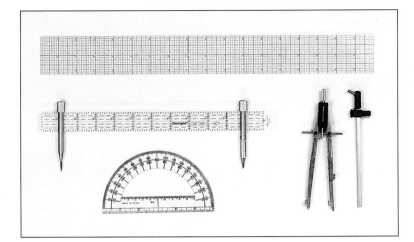

RULER, TWO KINDS OF
COMPASSES, AN EXTENDER,
AND A PROTRACTOR USED WHEN
DRAFTING RADIATING STARS.

Drafting Exercises

CIRCULAR STARS

Try the following exercise using a 6" square practice size. Once you know how to draft a basic star you can go on to any size and variation. Work with the graph paper on a pad of paper (so that the drafting compass point doesn't move) and keep your pencils sharp. Hold the drafting compass by the top, not the side arm. If you have trouble swinging the compass accurately, try holding it still and turning the paper under it.

Exercise 1: The Circular Star

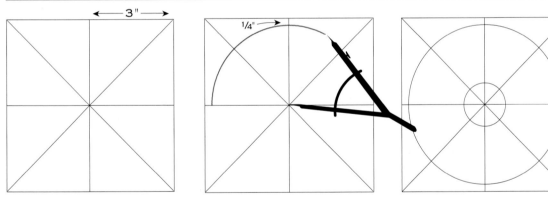

FIGURE 2.1   FIGURE 2.2   FIGURE 2.3

✧ *Drafting Points 1-4, Using a Regular (black) Pencil*

Step 1. Draw a 6" square with diagonal lines from the corners and horizontal and vertical lines in the center (at the 3" mark) of the block. (Figure 2.1)

Step 2. Set the drafting compass point in the center and the pencil/marker arm ¼" in from the top of the square. (The background is easier to piece if the star is allowed to float inside the block.) Swing the compass to make this outer circle. (Figure 2.2)

Step 3. Draw a 1½" circle in the middle of the square (it will have a ¾" radius). This is the <u>drafting circle</u> and will determine the width of the rays. A general rule is to start with a circle that is approximately one-quarter the diameter of the outer circle. A small circle will make thin rays; a larger circle will make fat rays. (Figure 2.3)

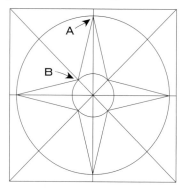

FIGURE 2.4

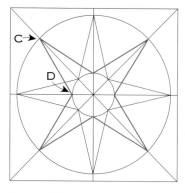

FIGURE 2.5

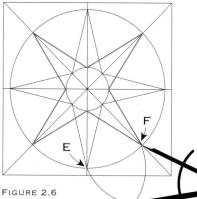

FIGURE 2.6

Step 4. Use a ruler to draw slanted lines from the outside circle at A to the inside circle at B to create the sides of the rays in the horizontal and vertical positions. (Figure 2.4)

✧ Drafting Points 5-8 Using a Red Pencil

Step 5. Draw slanted lines from the outside circle at C to the inside circle at D to create the sides of the rays in the diagonal positions. (Figure 2.5)

✧ Drafting Points 9-16 With the Bisecting Technique, Using a Blue Pencil

Step 6. Find the middle between two of the eight rays by bisecting the distance between E and F. Set the compass to the distance between E and F and swing the drafting compass from E into the area beyond the square and mark an arc. Move the drafting compass so that the point swings from F and mark an arc that crosses the previous one. (Figure 2.6)

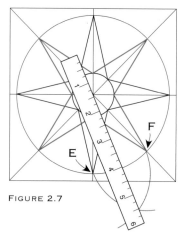

FIGURE 2.7

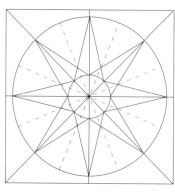

FIGURE 2.8

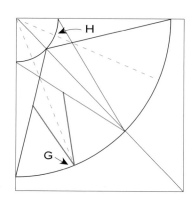

FIGURE 2.9

Step 7. Place the ruler along the line from the center point and the crossing of the arcs to mark a dashed line to show the new 16th-point position on the outer circle and the inner circle. This is called bisecting and can be used to accurately divide any curved space in half. (Figure 2.7)

Step 8. Repeat this procedure around the circle. (Figure 2.8)

Step 9. Use the ruler to draw new rays by laying the ruler on the blue mark "G" on the outer circle and on the blue mark "H" on the inner circle. The intersection "H" is offset from the ray by 45° and can be found by counting over two radiating lines on the inside circle in this first bisection. Mark a solid line from G to the edge of the adjoining ray (the first intersecting line). (Figure 2.9)

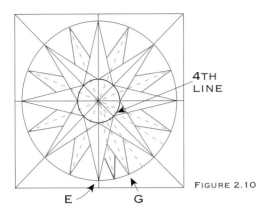

4TH
LINE

FIGURE 2.10

E   G

Step 10. Repeat this procedure around the circle to finish the 16 points.

✧ *Drafting Points 17-32 Using a Green Pencil*
Step 11. To further divide this star into 32 points, bisect again using the new distance between the E & G rays. Count over four radiating lines on the inner circle to find the angle for the new ray in the next (32-point) bisection. (Figure 2.10)

Traditional Mariner's Compass designs on quilts are commonly 16 to 32 points, although I have seen wonderful quilts with 64 points. A 16-point star has a spiky character and the addition of 16 more points (32) not only doubles the number of pieces in the design, but also tends to soften the star giving it a rounder character. You can double the number of any division (example: five to ten, six to 12) by using the bisecting technique.

VARIATIONS

At this stage of the drafting, you have all the lines necessary to create the pattern shapes for making a 16- or 32-point Star. It is not necessary to draft the complete design in order to have the pattern shapes for the templates.

However, it is helpful to have a complete design to help you visualize fabric placement and the piecing sequence. I have given names to the basic stars. The numbers identify the pattern pieces necessary to construct these basic stars.

Here are some variations on the theme:

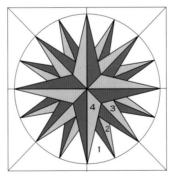

FIGURE 2.11
SPLIT STAR

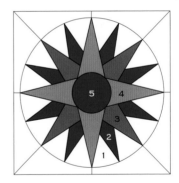

FIGURE 2.12
SUNBURST WITH 16 POINTS

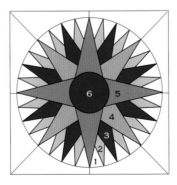

FIGURE 2.13
SUNBURST WITH 32 POINTS

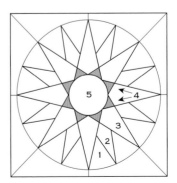

FIGURE 2.14
STARFLOWER

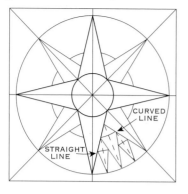

FIGURE 2.15

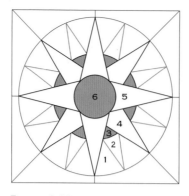

FIGURE 2.16

CONCENTRIC CIRCLE STAR

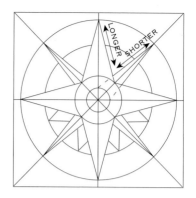

FIGURE 2.17

Another popular variation has the rays divided horizontally at the base. Use the compass to create a curved line or a ruler for a straight line. (Figure 2.15)

Variations are created by mixing different width rays or different length rays. (Figure 2.17) A new outer ring can be drawn, and the ends of some rays will touch this new, smaller circle.

A further variation is in the number of divisions in the star. The typical design that is called Mariner's Compass is divided like a navigational compass so that it has north, south, east, and west, based on the four points that can be divided into 8, 16, 32, or 64 points. Use a protractor to divide stars into other popular divisions based on five, six, or nine.

Exercise 2: Variations on the Simple Mariner's Compass

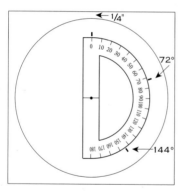

FIGURE 2.18

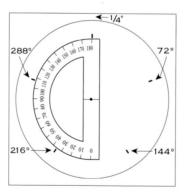

FIGURE 2.19

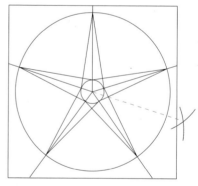

FIGURE 2.20

✧ Drafting a Star Divisible by Five.

Step 1. Draw a 6" square and find the center. Draw a circle ¼" inside the square. (Figure 2.18)

Step 2. Align the middle of the protractor (intersection of 90° and 0/180) with the center of the circle.

Step 3. Use the protractor to mark every 72° (72, 144, 216, 288, 0/360).
To mark points after 180°, reverse the protractor and use 180 less, i.e., for 216 use 36 (216–180=36). (Figure 2.19)

Step 4. Once you have divided the circle into five sections, draw a drafting circle and use the ruler to draw the sides of the rays. Use the bisecting technique on page 24 to further divide the spaces. (Figure 2.20)

✧ *Drafting a Star Divisible by Six.*

Use the instructions for dividing a star by five, but this time, mark every 60° (60, 120, 180, 240, 300, 0/360).

✧ *Drafting a Star Divisible by Nine.*

Use the instructions for dividing a star by five, but this time, mark every 40° (40, 80, 120, 160, 200, 240, 280, 320, 0/360).

It isn't necessary to draft the complete design for the traditional symmetrical star in order to have the pattern shapes required for the templates. However, it is helpful to have a complete design to help you visualize fabric placement and the piecing sequence.

OUTSIDE SHAPES

Circles are the traditional shape for radiating stars, probably because it is not difficult to piece the gently curving shape into background fabric. However it is certainly possible to draw the star into almost any shape as shown in Figure 2.21 and the photo below. When drafting the rays, the points should be drawn to the edge of your outside shape, just as you would for drafting a star in a circle.

SQUARE STAR,
25" x 25", 1994,
BY THE AUTHOR.
▶

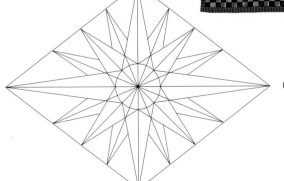

FIGURE 2.21

OVAL STARS

The oval is a graceful classic shape that quiltmakers admire. It is easy to piece into a background even though the piecing is more complex as the star has more pattern shapes, and reversals of the pattern pieces are necessary.

An oval is longer than it is wide. My advice is first to explore where you want to put this oval. You may already have the shape you need in an oval hoop, table top, silver tray or the dimensions of a double bed. Use that shape to determine the proportion of your oval (length and width). However, if you are starting from scratch, a good rule is to make the oval one half the distance longer than it is wide. Example: 20" x 30".

The most graceful oval maintains the relationship between the length and the width around the curve. There are a number of ways to draft the "perfect" oval. The paper tape method is my favorite.

Exercise 3: The Oval Star Using the Paper Tape Method

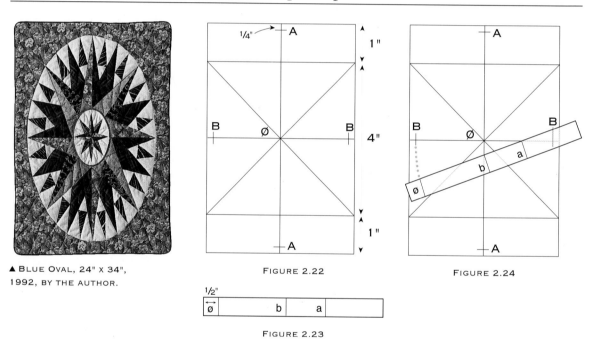

▲ BLUE OVAL, 24" x 34", 1992, BY THE AUTHOR.

FIGURE 2.22

FIGURE 2.24

FIGURE 2.23

Step 1. Cut a strip of paper ¹/₂" wide off the bottom of your graph paper to use later as your drafting tool.

Step 2. Draw a 4" square and make it into a rectangle by adding 1" at the top and 1" at the bottom.

Step 3. Mark diagonal lines through the corners of the square and horizontal/vertical lines through the middle of the rectangle. (Figure 2.22)

Step 4. Mark positions ¹/₄" inside the rectangle to establish where the oval will float inside the rectangle. Name those positions A and B with Ø as the center.

Step 5. On the strip of paper tape, mark ¹/₂" from the end as the lowercase letter ø; then mark the distance from Ø to B (name it with a lowercase b) and Ø to A (name it with a lowercase a). (Figure 2.23)

Step 6. Use the paper tape to make a series of dots that can be connected to create the oval. (Figure 2.24) Begin by placing the paper tape on the horizontal line so that ø is at B and b is at Ø. Now move the tape down line A while keeping the "b" on line A and the "a" on line B and mark points at the ø. Continue moving the tape and making marks at "ø". (Figure 2.25)

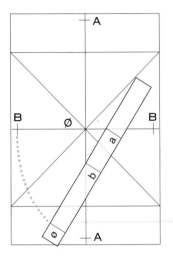

FIGURE 2.25

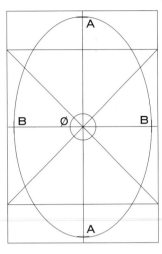

FIGURE 2.26

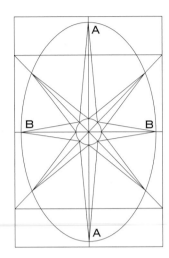

FIGURE 2.27

Step 7. Mark the complete oval or fold and trace to repeat the second half. (Figure 2.26)

Step 8. To draft a star inside the oval, choose either a circle or oval for the center and refer back to the drafting section's Step 4 on page 24. To mark for further divisions use a protractor.

Another way to mark for further divisions is to use a ruler as shown in Figure 2.28. Place the ruler on the intersections C and D, and draw a line through these two intersections.

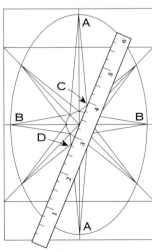

FIGURE 2.28

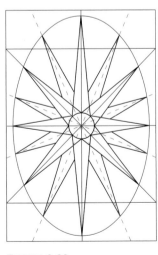

FIGURE 2.29
CIRCLE CENTER

FIGURE 2.30
OVAL CENTER

Templates for a symmetrical star in an oval can be done in the traditional way, but I have found that the freezer paper template method drafted full-size works very well because of the number of pieces and the reversals (see Pullout Section at the back of this book).

Exercise 4: Off-Center Star

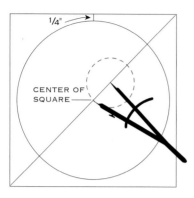

FIGURE 2.31

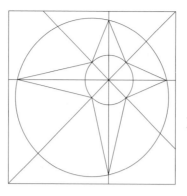

FIGURE 2.32

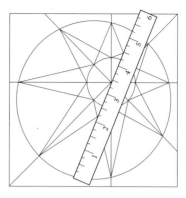

FIGURE 2.33

The radiating lines in the star can be placed off-center in any shape desired.

Step 1. Draw a 6" square and mark the center point and one diagonal. Set the drafting compass pointer in the center with the pencil/marker arm ¼" in from the square. Swing the compass to make the outer circle. (Figure 2.31)

Step 2. Set the compass to ¾" and set the pencil/marker arm in the center with the pointer arm up the diagonal line to the right. Swing from the compass pointer so that the drafting circle is off-center. (Figure 2.31)

Step 3. Draw horizontal and vertical lines through the new center using the straight edge of the square block to position your ruler. The remaining diagonal line is drawn at a right angle (90°) to the first diagonal. Use a vertical line on your ruler as a reference to line up the first diagonal. (Figure 2.32)

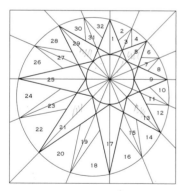

FIGURE 2.34

Step 4. Continue with the star drafting as in Step 4 on page 24.

Step 5. Divide for new ray positions using a ruler.

All of the variations discussed so far can be applied to this star. Since there are so many pattern pieces in the off-center variations, the freezer paper template technique works well. Just remember to number the pieces the same as your original design if you trace onto template material or freezer paper. Make a "map" if you draft directly onto the freezer paper.

If you draft onto the dull side of the freezer paper, your design will be *reversed* when it is assembled and sewn. If you find this confusing, draw the design on the shiny side of the freezer paper with a thin permanent pen. Label the pieces on both shiny and dull sides. See Chapter Four for more information.

After you have practiced the basic drafting exercises, you are ready to design your full-size star. Clear the table top or drafting surface off and assemble your tools, sharp pencils, and full-size paper. Choose from all the design variations discussed and begin to create your own original star.

Checklist of Possible Variations When Drafting Stars That Radiate From a Center

1. **Size:** How big do you want your star to be?

2. **Outside Shape:** Will it be round, oval, square, hexagonal, triangular, etc.?

3. **Inside Drafting Shape:** Round or oval?

4. **Position of Inside Drafting Shape:** Will it be in the center, off-center up, off-center right, etc.?

5. **Number of Basic Divisions:** Four, five, six, eight, or nine?.

6. **Width of the Rays:** Will they be wide or narrow? This is determined by the size of the *inside* drafting shape.

7. **Length of the Rays:** This is determined by the *outside* shape.

8. **Divisions Within the Rays:** Are they vertical (split), horizontal (concentric circle), diagonal (Starflower), etc.? See pages 25 and 26 of this chapter.

If you are drafting a traditional symmetrical set of patterns, then make a full-size drawing of the design with all of the pieces that will be necessary to make the templates. You can use the drafting compass or dividers to check the length of both sides of each ray or piecing wedge to be sure all fit together accurately. Dividers look like a compass, but they have two sharp points (no pencil is used). They are more accurate than a traditional compass.

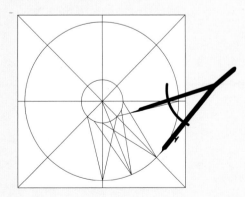

FIGURE 2.35

If you are drafting or tracing one-time-only patterns onto freezer paper be sure that they are numbered to match your original design or a smaller "map" that reminds you how they fit together.

Chapter Three
Fabric Selection

Quiltmakers have come to prefer 100%-cotton fabric because it is the easiest to use. Select fabrics that are similar in nature, and avoid fabrics that are loosely woven. Quilters have differing opinions about whether fabrics should be prewashed or used right from the bolt. Either way, be sure to test for bleeding, as the fabric may encounter water or steam at some time during the construction process.

Test for bleeding by wetting a small sample of the fabric. Put it on a white paper towel or white cloth and allow it to dry. If there is significant color transfer, wash the fabric. If it still bleeds after washing, select another fabric.

The hardest part of making a quilt (as well as the most exciting) is selecting the fabric. I often hear quilters say that the color is the hardest part. For me the fabric choice includes the variables of color and value as well as texture, scale, style, etc., if it is a print. I tend to let my emotions guide me in choices of color. Most quilters won't work with colors they don't like, and you can usually trust yourself in this area. However, this is not to say that studying color won't improve your work and give you confidence.

The contrast of value (the amount of light and dark) is the thing that seems most important to me in this design.

Much of the charm of these stars is in the crisp, thin nature of the long rays and contrast of value is what makes them work.

▲ HOME FOR THE HOLIDAYS (DETAIL), 57" x 60", 1994, BY LISA ANN CARRILLO, WOODLAND HILLS, CALIFORNIA.

PATH BY
TWILIGHT,
82" X 82",
1993,
BY SHARON
COMMINS,
LOS ANGELES,
CALIFORNIA.
◄

Sharon Commins has deliberately chosen to submerge her stars into the background of *Path by Twilight* so that you almost have to search for them. She made an artistic decision in favor of subtlety.

If you want your stars to show prominently, start by planning the background fabric and then select fabrics that will show up on it after they have been reduced to sharp-pointed rays.

To experiment with your choices, fold the fabrics diagonally twice and then overlap them onto the background fabric in the same order and general arrangement in which they will appear after they are sewn.

This will give you a chance to see if the value differences hold when they are reduced to sharply pointed rays.

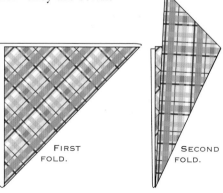

FIRST FOLD.

SECOND FOLD.

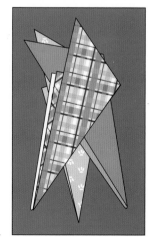

FIGURE 3.1

FIGURE 3.2

FIGURE 3.3

The fabric in the pie-shaped background pieces will normally change grain line as they move around the circle. (Figure 3.2)

Select a fabric that has a non-directional print if you want the circle of the star to blend in with the background in the block. (Figure 3.3)

If it is important that the print direction match that of the rest of the background, use the freezer paper template method of construction. It is very easy to mark the grain line on the freezer-paper templates for each individual piece using this method.

Quiltmakers often choose light-value backgrounds because they allow the broadest choices of color, but I favor dark backgrounds because they make the stars sparkle!

▲ OVAL MARINER'S COMPASS,
20" x 30", 1994,
BY YOKO NOMURA,
NORTHRIDGE, CALIFORNIA.

▲ MADRAS STAR, 35" x 38", 1992, BY THE AUTHOR.

It is certainly possible to use a range of different fabrics in similar values for the background of the stars.

Madras Star has a variety of similar value prints used in the background color as does the star by Lisa Ann Carrillo in the detail at the beginning of this chapter, on page 32.

Starfire has a changing variety of value and colors across the background. (See cover, page 18, and Pattern 9.)

▲ NAUTICAL STARS,
73" x 88", 1986,
BY THE AUTHOR.

Another approach is to use changing values in the background as seen in *Nautical Stars*. This can be quite a challenge as you must change the values of the fabrics used in the rays as the values change in the background.

ARCTIC STAR,
61" x 61",
1993,
BY THE AUTHOR.
◄

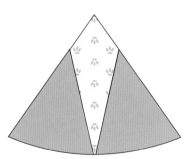

FIGURE 3.4

FIGURE 3.5

The fabrics used in the rays can be more varied than the background, but there is not a lot of area in the skinny rays. Put larger scale fabrics in the larger rays. If a fabric has areas where the print is the same value as the background, be careful that it does not occur at the tip of the ray. The similar value area of the print can blend with the background and make the tip appear blunted. (Figure 3.4)

Directional fabric such as stripes and plaids can add a lot of energy to the design, and you can control the placement by following the angles of the ray or ignore it as the mood strikes you. (Figure 3.5)

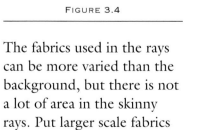

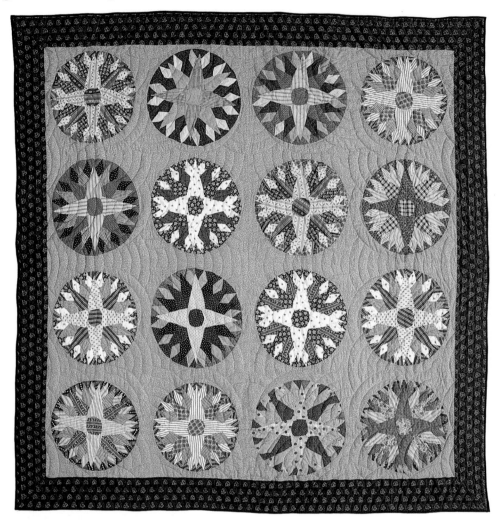

CHIPS AND
WHETSTONES,
80" x 80",
CIRCA 1880,
PENNSYLVANIA.
COLLECTION OF
THE AUTHOR.

◄

CHIPS AND WHETSTONES
(DETAIL).

If you have selected a design with a circle in the center, try to chose fabrics that give a positive effect. Avoid fabrics that have the same value as the background or the circle will tend to "drop out" and look like a hole as seen in this detail of an antique quilt from Pennsylvania. The design in this quilt is sometimes called Chips and Whetstones. Several of the rays disappear and create fishtails or rockets because they are cut from fabric that has a similar value as the background wedge.

Fabrics with the same value as the background are good choices for designs that have a star in the center. The center star will appear to "float" over the background.

▲ COMPASS ROSES, 65" x 65", 1990, BY MARLENE PETERMAN, WEST HILLS, CALIFORNIA, AND THE AUTHOR.

You might also choose a design with horizontal divisions in the rays as you appear to be able to "look through" the star into the background. The stars in *Compass Roses* have a light, lacy appearance.

I've given my reasons for choosing fabrics in certain situations, but there is always a good reason for doing just the opposite. My basic advice for fabric selections is first to decide the relative value of the fabrics. Can you actually detect the difference between the fabrics that are being placed next to each other?

If you aren't happy with the color, see if you can throw in a little of the complementary color—the opposite color on the color wheel. This will often spark up the color. Most quilters agree that it is the fabric that draws them to this craft, and the personal way that we use it is what keeps us excited about the quilts that we make.

Chapter Four
Construction

No matter how inspiring your design and how wonderfully effective your fabric choices, you probably won't be happy with the results if your construction skills don't meet the challenge. The beauty of this design lies in those sharp and sometimes skinny rays. So the most important aspect of Mariner's Compass construction is accuracy, accuracy, accuracy.

The traditional method of making templates and marking fabric works very well if you sew accurately through the intersections and don't let the many bias edges stretch. I still find this the best method for hand piecing the traditional designs.

Freezer paper templates can be used to advantage in patterns that have many different shapes (off-center stars). This method enables you to easily keep track of the location of each piece. It also seems to stabilize the bias edges and prevents them from stretching during the sewing process. The process takes about the same amount of time as traditional piecing, but your time is used in different ways.

Sewing onto paper foundations involves sewing directly through paper patterns. It produces very accurate results as well as giving great success with very small piecing units such as miniatures. The paper helps to stabilize the fabric. This method can only be used efficiently in designs that reduce to pieceable segments. It can often be used in combination with the freezer paper template technique.

Traditional Template Piecing

Many of the patterns in this book show a sewing line and cutting line with a $\frac{1}{4}$" seam allowance in between them. Some quilters prefer to make their templates using the finished size of the piece. The shape is marked on the wrong side of the fabric, and $\frac{1}{4}$" is added to the shape when it is cut. Others prefer to make templates that are the cut size of the shape including seam allowances. The pattern is marked on the wrong side of the fabric, and the sewing line is marked $\frac{1}{4}$" inside the cutting line. The sewing line may also be determined by sewing along the edge of a $\frac{1}{4}$" presser foot or following a mark on the throat plate of a sewing machine.

MAKING TEMPLATES

Make templates by tracing accurately onto clear plastic with a thin permanent pen or trace the pattern onto paper and then glue onto cardboard or plastic. Be sure to include all of the information such as name of pattern, letter, number of pieces to be cut, grain line, reversal information, and any matching marks. If you have access to a photocopy machine that makes accurate reproductions (doesn't distort or change the size), you can copy the patterns and then glue them to a stiff material.

It is helpful on templates that include seam allowances to punch a small hole ($\frac{1}{16}$" to $\frac{1}{8}$") in the intersections with a paper punch or the end of a drafting compass. Mark a small dot through the hole on the fabric pieces with a pencil or other marking tool to aid in matching the shapes correctly. I generally cut the tips off the templates $\frac{1}{4}$" from the top and bottom to remind me where the intersections actually are.

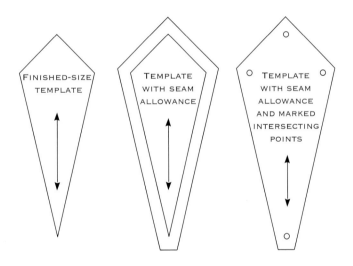

MARKING AND CUTTING WITH TEMPLATES

Lay the template on the back of the fabric following the suggested grain lines unless the fabric dictates some change. Use a marking pencil that will show on the fabric and mark around the template. Cut the fabric using scissors or a rotary cutter.

It is possible to cut up to four thicknesses of fabric if the fabric is non-directional. Make sure the fabric is smooth and pressed together. Hold your scissors or rotary cutter straight to prevent beveling.

The star designs are often enhanced with splits that have dark and light vertically or horizontally through the ray. In some cases the template can be cut from fabric which has been pre-sewn or printed. (Figures 4.2 and 4.3)

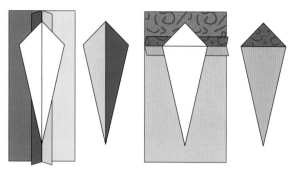

FIGURE 4.2, PRE-SEWN FABRIC

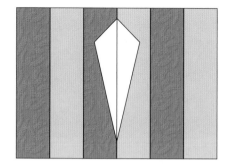

FIGURE 4.3, PRINTED FABRIC

SEWING

I usually use neutral colors such as black, white and shades of gray when stitching. Since the seams of the rays cross over each other, I generally select a thread value which is similar to the fabric of the rays and not the background fabric.

Keep in mind that the sides of the pieces are bias and can easily stretch; handle them carefully. Pin at the intersections and ease if the fabric has stretched. If you are hand piecing, stitch with small even stitches. There should be a $\frac{1}{4}$" seam allowance left at the tip of the ray point after it is stitched. If you are hand piecing, be sure to close up the seam at the tip. If you are sewing on the machine, the seam allowances will be stitched all the way through. This keeps the points sharp when the circles are joined to the background.

General Piecing Sequence

The star designs are pieced similarly with only slight differences.

Split Rays

Split ray variations are of two types. If the design meets in the center with eight seams, they can be constructed as shown in Figure 4.4, cutting only the smallest and largest rays from pre-sewn fabric as shown in Figure 4.2.

FIGURE 4.4

If the center is joined with a circle, the splits should all be cut from pre-sewn fabrics as shown in Figure 4.2 then assembled as shown in Figure 4.6. The circular center is appliquéd last (see page 53).

FIGURE 4.5

Concentric Circles

With concentric circle variations, the triangles at the base of the ray are pieced on first to complete the ray or the whole ray can be cut from pre-sewn fabric as shown in Figure 4.2.

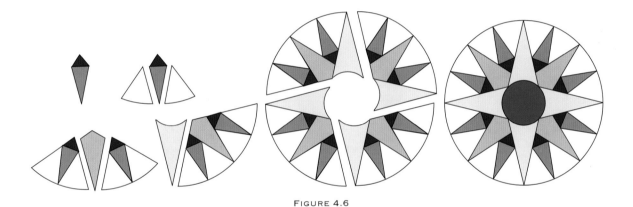

FIGURE 4.6

Sunburst

Sunburst variations can be pieced into asymmetrical quarters and the centers can be appliquéd or pieced last.

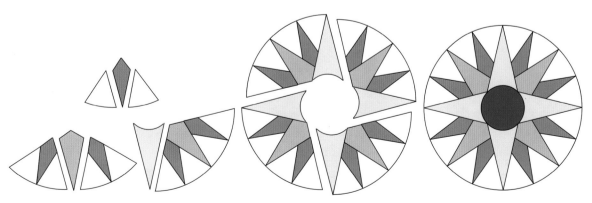

FIGURE 4.7

Starflower

For the Starflower variation, the small triangles in the center are pieced to the base of the largest ray as in Figure 4.8 and sewn as a diagonal wedge.

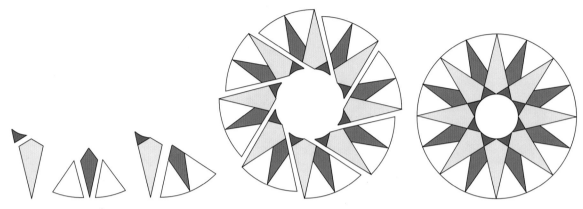

FIGURE 4.8

An alternate method is to sew the small triangles to both sides of the horizontal/vertical rays and then continue as shown in Figure 4.9.

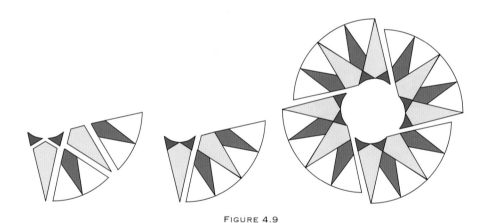

FIGURE 4.9

Freezer Paper Templates

This technique involves using templates made with freezer paper (paper with a light coating of plastic). Each piece of the design requires its own paper template, and it is ironed onto the back of the fabric. Templates are made without seam allowances—the template is for the sewing line so seam allowances must be added to the fabric piece before it is cut.

The patterns for the Off-Center Star and the ovals lend themselves particularly well to this technique because they have so many different pieces. You can also use this method on the traditional symmetrical stars, but each fabric piece requires its own paper template.

Designs Where Each Piece Is Unique (off-center and oval designs)

Step 1. Draft or trace your pattern directly onto a piece of freezer paper. Normally, I mark on the dull side of the freezer paper. If your pattern has reversals, marking on the dull side will cause the finished design to be reversed. Marking on the shiny side with a thin permanent pen will avoid confusion.

Step 2. Mark each piece of freezer paper with a letter or number that corresponds to a similarly marked diagram (your map!). It is also a good idea to mark grain line information and fabric choices on each piece before you cut them apart.

Step 3. Carefully cut the pattern pieces apart on the lines, and sort according to fabric.

Step 4. Proceed to Fabric Preparation on page 46.

Designs With Repeating Template (symmetrical round designs)

Step 1. Make cardboard or plastic templates without seam allowances for each unique pattern piece. Use a thin permanent pen to mark around the templates on the freezer paper the number of times you will need each pattern or trace the patterns directly from the book. Cut out each piece accurately by cutting on the inside of the marked line.

It is possible to speed up the process by stacking sheets of freezer paper to cut multiples of the same shape, but you must mark and cut carefully to avoid inaccuracies.

✧ *Example: Mariner's Compass With 16 Points (pattern on page 62)*

Step 1. Divide the number of templates for each repeating piece by four and trace this number of pieces onto freezer paper. (Figure 4.10)

Step 2. Cut three other pieces of paper the same size and stack (dull side to shiny side).

Step 3. Tack the pieces of freezer paper together with the tip of a hot iron about ½" inside each large piece in several places and in the center of the small pieces. (Figure 4.11)

Step 4. Cut through the four pieces of freezer paper accurately with scissors or a rotary cutter. Carefully pull the freezer papers apart.

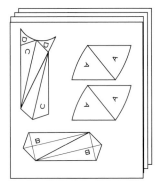

FIGURE 4.10

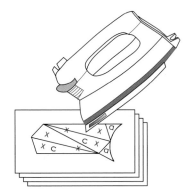

FIGURE 4.11

FABRIC PREPARATION

Step 1. Iron the freezer paper with the shiny side down to the *back* of the selected fabrics leaving ¾" of space between each piece. Be sure to use a hot **dry** iron.

Step 2. Cut out each piece roughly. Be sure there is more than ¼" around each piece.

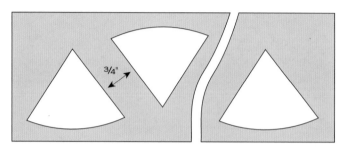

FIGURE 4.12

Step 3. Trim each piece leaving ¼" around each piece. It is most accurate to measure and cut the seam allowance with the rotary cutter and ruler or mark on the fabric using a ruler and then cut with scissors. (Figure 4.13)

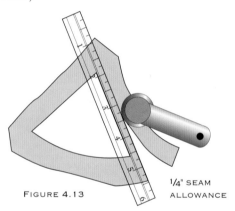

FIGURE 4.13

¼" SEAM
ALLOWANCE

Step 4. Mark each intersection with a dot on the fabric at the edge of the paper to use as a sewing reference later when you remove the paper from one side, or in case the paper should come loose during handling. Also mark on the fabric along the curved edges to create a sewing line that will be visible after the freezer paper is removed. (Figure 4.14)

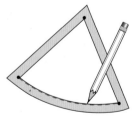

FIGURE 4.14

If the freezer paper has started to come loose during the cutting, iron the paper on again.

Off-center or oval designs have reversals. Be careful to arrange them for assembly from the same side as your example or map. The pieces will not fit together if you try to assemble them reversed.

SEWING

The illustrations in this chapter show the thread color as red so that you can differentiate it from the other colors and values in the drawing. I usually use neutral colors such as black, white and shades of gray when stitching. Since the seams of the rays cross over each other, I generally select a thread value which is similar to the fabric of the rays and not the background fabric.

The freezer paper can be saved and used again if you are careful not to sew through it during assembly. It is possible to stitch the seams with the freezer paper on both sides, but I find that I am more successful if I remove it from one side before I stitch. The general rule is to pin the pieces together at the intersections and then remove the freezer paper from the *underneath* side before you begin to sew. Try not to sew through the paper. Paper can be removed from stitched seams, but if it is a regular length stitch, the seam tends to distort as the paper is pulled out. If you are regularly sewing through paper it is best to shorten the length of your stitch (20 per inch) or use a larger than normal needle (size 14/90). This perforates the paper so that it pulls off more easily.

Machine Piecing

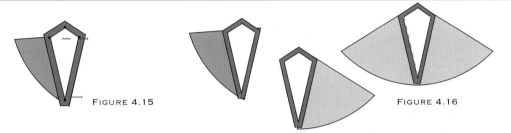

FIGURE 4.15   FIGURE 4.16

Step 1. Pin at the intersection, top, and bottom, and line up edges of fabric. (Figure 4.15)

Step 2. Carefully remove freezer paper on one side (pie-shaped piece) and sew along freezer paper from end to end, including through the seam allowances. Finger press the seam toward the background fabric (pie shape) and away from the sharply pointed ray. The paper helps the fabric to press well and keeps it from stretching. (Figure 4.16)

Step 3. Continue to pin, sew, and finger press following the assembly diagram for the type of star you are making. Remove alternate pieces of freezer paper as you go so that you do not have two pieces of paper under the needle at a time. Be sure to save all of the freezer paper templates even if you don't plan to use them again. You might change your mind about a fabric or even make a mistake and need to recut something. When the star is complete, remove all of the freezer paper.

Hand Piecing

The method is the same, but the paper tends to make the handling during the sewing feel awkward at first because of the stiffness of the paper. Be sure to remove the paper piece from one side as this makes it easier to sew.

Combining Methods

See page 51 for information on how to combine the freezer paper template method with paper foundations to easily add details within the basic Mariner's Compass. You can add an extra set of points, the triangles around the center circle or concentric circle variations.

Paper Foundation

Some of the star designs can be sewn directly onto a paper foundation using a sew-and-flip method. The star is divided into pieceable segments and a full-size paper pattern is prepared for each segment.

There are two approaches to this method. One is to cut fabric into strips or chunks and trim as you assemble. If you find it necessary to control the grain line of the pieces use the second method which involves precutting the pieces into approximate size shapes before you begin stitching.

The paper foundation method gives remarkable accuracy, and the skinny fabric rays are stabilized during the sewing process so there is little stretching of bias edges. However the paper must be removed at the completion of the project and the method may use more fabric than traditional methods.

You can trace the patterns or make photocopies for each segment. A clever way to make multiple copies is to stack layers of paper with the original and then "sew" through the lines with your sewing machine and an empty needle. The needle pierces the paper and "copies" the design. I have also used a pierced paper pattern as a stencil and rubbed colored chalk through it to create more copies. The thinner and crisper the paper, the easier it will be to remove after sewing.

Check for distortion. All copies must be made from the same original so that they fit together when completed. You can copy with your sewing machine as described above.

Some people like to trace the design onto freezer paper so that the fabric sticks to the shiny side of the freezer paper when it is flipped and pressed. If you have access to a photocopy machine, you can copy directly onto freezer paper if you are careful. Cut pieces of freezer paper the size of a regular piece of photocopy paper. Put a piece of regular paper against the shiny side of the freezer paper and tack it together at the top with an iron. Run this set of papers through the manual feed of the copier, so the regular paper is the one that touches the hot roller as they leave the machine. The regular paper keeps the plastic coating on the freezer paper from sticking to the hot roller. Remove the regular paper.

Using the paper foundation method, you will be positioning the fabric on the back side of the pattern, then stitching through the fabric/paper layers on the front side of the paper pattern using the marked lines. Remember to set your sewing machine stitch length to short (about 20 stitches per inch) for paper piecing so that the needle will pierce the paper often and allow easy removal of the paper. Using a larger needle (90/14) will also help pierce the paper. The pattern will be reversed.

✧ *Example: Eight-point Star (pattern is given here)*
The pattern for this practice star will fit in the center of the Off-Center Star or Oval Star in the pullout section and in Plaid Mariner's Compass (pattern on page 65).

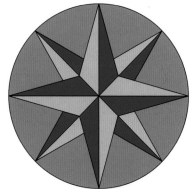

FIGURE 4.17

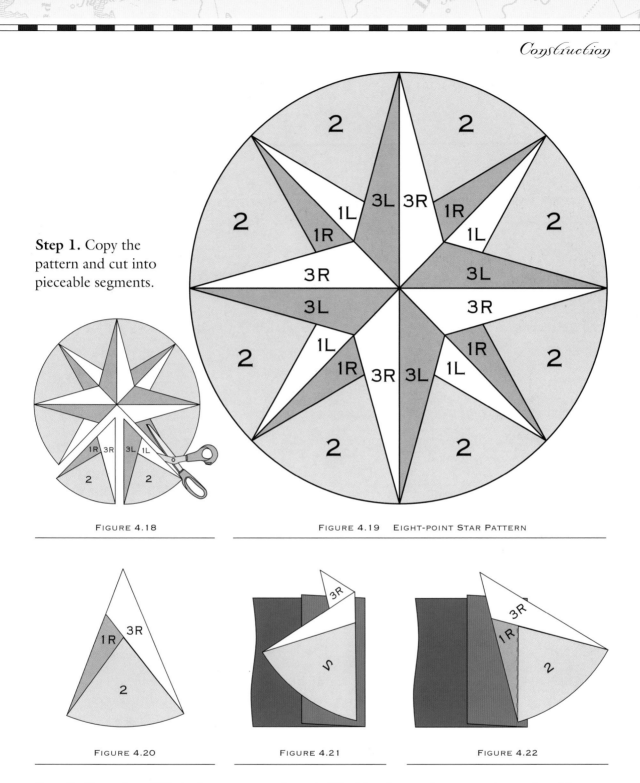

Step 1. Copy the pattern and cut into pieceable segments.

FIGURE 4.18

FIGURE 4.19   EIGHT-POINT STAR PATTERN

FIGURE 4.20

FIGURE 4.21

FIGURE 4.22

Step 2. Cut strips of fabric that are approximately 1" wider than each pattern piece at its widest part.

Step 3. Place the dark and light strips for piece #1R and #2 right sides together and position them on the back side of the paper with the fabric over the center line $1/4$" on the darker side. Be sure to allow enough fabric to extend beyond the ends of pattern piece #1R to allow for the seam allowance. You can check to see that there is sufficient fabric for #2 by folding the paper back over the fabric. (Figure 4.21)

Step 4. Stitch through the center line in pattern piece #1R. (Figure 4.22)

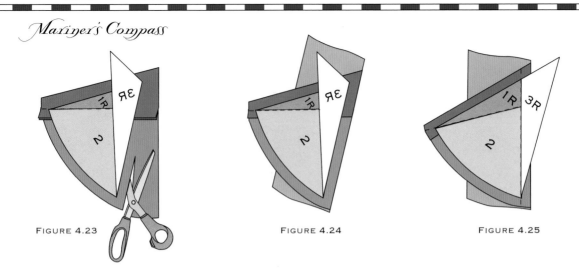

FIGURE 4.23   FIGURE 4.24   FIGURE 4.25

Step 5. Press fabrics and trim with scissors to allow ¼" seam allowance around #1R and #2. Fold the paper pattern at the edges of #3R to get a guide line to trim the fabric for the seam allowances. (Figure 4.23)

Step 6. Select a new strip of fabric for Piece #3 and position it on the back side of the paper pattern lining the edge up with the trimmed seam of #1R/#2. (Figure 4.24) Check to see that there is sufficient fabric by folding paper piece #3R back over.

Step 7. Stitch. Then press. Trim to allow ¼" seam allowance. (Figure 4.25)

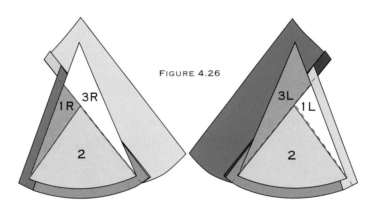

FIGURE 4.26

In this example, you will have stitched one-eighth of the design. The remaining seven pie-shaped pieces must then be made. Notice that four will be right-hand elements of the design and four will be left-hand elements. (Figure 4.27)

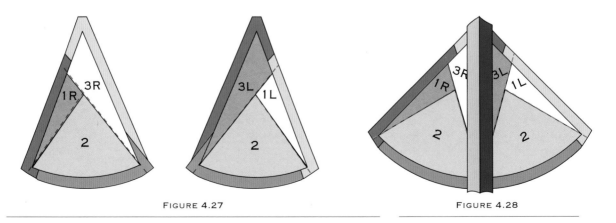

FIGURE 4.27   FIGURE 4.28

Step 8. Leave the paper on the fabric until all of the stitching on all eight units is complete. Sew a right-hand unit to a left-hand unit along side 3 (R and L). Press the seam allowances between the units open so that you can get the best intersections in the middle where eight pieces of fabric will intersect. Repeat three times. (Figure 4.28)

Step 9. Sew two sections together for each half of the block; then sew the halves together to complete the star. The completed block will be the reverse image of the pattern.

If you wish to control the direction of the fabric grain line, do not use strips or chunks of fabric. Precut the pattern pieces using a slightly larger seam allowance (approximately $^3/_8$") and follow the sequence of piecing.

To remove the paper, crumple and gently rub between your fists before you pull the paper off. Folding the paper and fabric at the seams also helps to release it. Use a seam ripper or small scissors to open up large areas of paper so that you can take a hold of the paper to peel it away from the seams.

Combination Methods

If you are using freezer paper template methods to make the star it is possible to combine it with the paper foundation method to speedily add some details. Be sure to reduce the size of your stitch to 20 to the inch or change to a larger needle before you sew through paper foundations and then remember to increase the stitch length when you go back to regular stitching.

Method 1. Precut Shapes

Make cardboard templates with seam allowances and precut the fabric for the rays and triangles. You don't have to make them extremely accurate.

Position the precut ray to the back of the pattern wedge and pin (or iron if it is freezer paper). Line up the background piece to the ray fabric and stitch through both fabric and paper on the line. Seam should include the $^1/_4$" seam allowance at each end of the seam. (Figure 4.29)

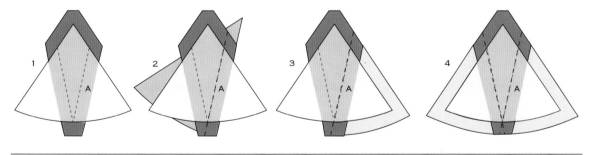

FIGURE 4.29

Method 2. Cut Strips or Large Pieces of Fabric and Trim As You Go.

Pin or iron (freezer paper) a strip or large piece of fabric to the back of the paper pattern. Fold the paper back on the stitching line and trim fabric to $\frac{1}{4}$" seam allowance. Position the companion fabric to the trimmed edge and stitch on the line. Trim the fabric to fit the paper shape leaving $\frac{1}{4}$" seam allowance. (Figure 4.30)

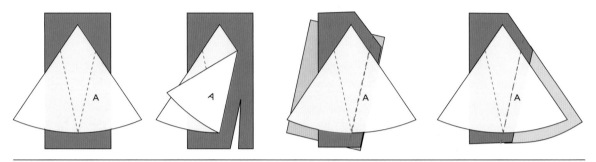

FIGURE 4.30

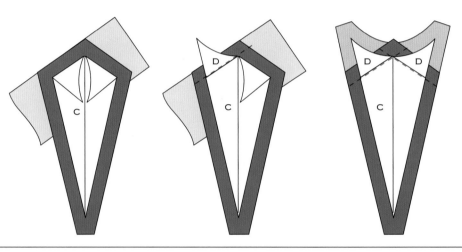

FIGURE 4.31

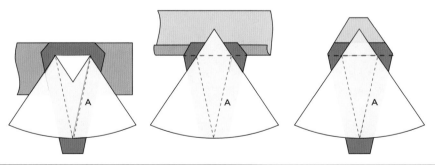

FIGURE 4.32

After these segments have been pieced using the paper foundation method, return to the freezer paper template method for the rest of the star. Remember to change the stitch length on your sewing machine. The example shown is for the **32-point Mariner's Compass Star.**

Finishing the Round Center

Center circles could be pieced, but I prefer to appliqué them to insure that they are round.

Method 1. Prepare a paper template the size of the desired circle. Pin it to the back of the fabric and cut around the circle leaving ¼" seam allowance. Baste through the paper and fabric. (Figure 4.33) Fold the circle into quarters to make matching marks and pin it to the pieced star block. Appliqué with matching thread. Remove the top basting, cut away the back fabric if necessary, and remove the paper.

Method 2. Freezer paper also makes a good template. Iron the shiny side of the paper to the back of the fabric and cut it out leaving ¼" seam allowance. Pull the freezer paper off and pin it with the shiny side up to the back of the fabric. Use the tip of a hot iron to press the seam allowances to the template as shown. (Figure 4.34) Remove the freezer paper. Fold the circle into quarters to make matching marks and pin it to the pieced star block. Appliqué with matching thread.

SHINY SIDE OF
FREEZER PAPER

FIGURE 4.33 METHOD 1   FIGURE 4.34 METHOD 2

Pressing and Blocking

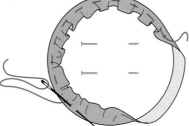

As the sewing progresses using traditional machine piecing, you will need to press the seam allowances. Use a dry iron and press as illustrated. Hand pieced blocks can be pressed after the sewing is completed. Paper foundation and freezer paper template blocks can be pressed with a dry iron or finger pressed during the assembly. Be sure to press the seam allowances *away* from the tips of the rays.

The major problem with radiating star designs is their tendency to form volcano or funnel shapes after they are stitched instead of nice flat circles. It is hard to cut all those pieces accurately from fabric which tends to distort and then sew them back together so that you still have 360 degrees left in your circle. It is especially hard using the sewing machine, which puts a certain amount of tension into the stitched seam. So I always block the stars. It helps to completely open the seams and encourages the star to flatten.

You will need a flat surface which will take pins. An ironing board will work well for small stars. If you don't have a large pin board, then lay a towel on a firm carpeted surface. Pin the star to the flat surface beginning with the tips of the vertical rays and then the horizontal rays, easing them flat. Continue around the circle pinning opposing points until the star is flat. Press with a steam iron. Do not remove from the pin board until the fabric is cool and dry. If the star is too small to iron, pin to the board, spray with a fine mist of water and allow to dry.

Attaching Stars to the Background

If you have pieced the star into a circle there are three basic ways to get it into a background.

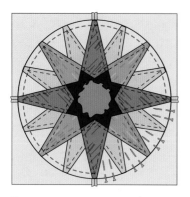

FIGURE 4.36
METHOD 1

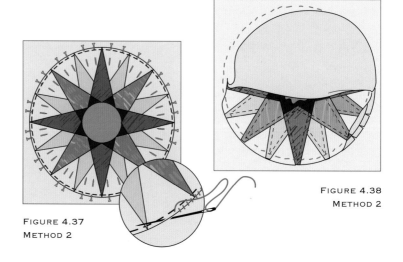

FIGURE 4.37
METHOD 2

FIGURE 4.38
METHOD 2

METHODS:

1. Piece it into a background block. This is the most time and fabric efficient method.

Prepare four quarter circle background pieces and sew them together. Pin the star into the background using the matching marks for the points of the rays of the star and then sew. (Figure 4.36)

2. Appliqué it to the background. This allows for positioning the star anywhere on a quilt top.

Baste the seam allowances on the star circle under $\frac{1}{4}$" and pin in desired position on quilt top. Appliqué by hand with small stitches using matching thread. (Figure 4.37)

Remove the top basting and cut the background fabric away from behind the block, leaving a $\frac{1}{4}$" seam allowance. Clip this seam if necessary and press away from the star. (Figure 4.38)

3. Appliqué-baste and machine piece. This allows for positioning the star anywhere on quilt top and for machine piecing the circle.

Baste seam allowances under as for appliqué. Pin to the background and, using a blind stitch, baste the circle to the background with $\frac{1}{2}$" stitches. Remove the top basting, cut the background from behind the circle, and use the blind stitch basting as a guide to machine or hand piecing. (Figure 4.39) Clip this seam if necessary and press away from the star.

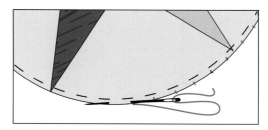

FIGURE 4.39 METHOD 3

STARSHINE,
34" × 34",
1994,
BY THE
AUTHOR.

◀

FIGURE 4.40

FIGURE 4.41

It is possible to overlap the stars as seen in *Starshine* above and *Night Lights* page 14. Lay the basted circles over each other making sure that the rays do not overlap each other. (Figure 4.40)

Sew the stars into the background using either Method 2 or 3 on previous page. Slash through the background to reveal the ray underneath and reverse appliqué the seam allowances to the edges of the underneath ray. (Figure 4.41)

Be sure to use matching thread, very small appliqué stitches and extra stitches at the inside cut so the background fabric won't ravel.

Quilting

A goal in planning the quilting is to have relatively similar amounts of quilting throughout the piece. An immediately obvious quilting design is one which radiates in the same way as the star. A problem can sometime occur here if the piecing is creating a volcano, then the quilting should help to control it and not encourage it. If you choose this kind of quilting design make sure that all the lines do not come all the way into the center. (Figure 4.42)

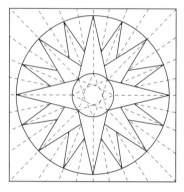 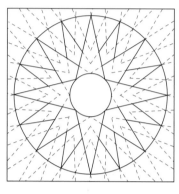 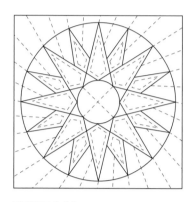

FIGURE 4.42   FIGURE 4.43   FIGURE 4.44

The star designs lend themselves well to structural quilting, or quilting within the pieces themselves. Since the seam allowances have been pressed away from the tips it is easy to quilt inside the rays themselves near the seam allowances or measure in $\frac{1}{2}$".

Large stars with more area in the rays may need to have extra fill patterns. See *Starfire* on page 18 and the cover for some ideas. The angles of the smaller rays on the stars can be continued through the larger rays or new rays can be added.

Figure 4.43 shows quilting lines extending out both sides of the ends of the rays. See *Twilight Star* page 88. Figure 4.44 shows quilting out the points of the rays along one side of the seam creating a spiral. More divisions can be added between the points to enhance the spiral effect. See *Epicenter* page 19 and *Cartwheel Costa Rica* page 80.

Background fill behind the star is very important. It can be traditional as shown in *Plaid Mariners Compass* page 65 (uneven cross hatch), meandering in *Broderie Perse Mariner's Compass* page 74 or follow the design in the fabric as seen in *Starshine* on page 55.

The star design itself would make a good quilting design for an alternate block or as shown in the center of *Ocean Waves* with a fleur-de-lis border page 57.

Labels

The more documentation you give your work the more value potential owners will give it. So be sure to sign and date your work in some permanent way. Embroidery or permanent ink signatures on the front are good, but an extra touch is to make a special label for the back. I had an extra block left from *Starfire* page 18 so I added it to the back and signed and dated it in the center circle.

Velma McCabe made an elegant, informative label for her *Santa Maria* page 4 by designing an anchor and embellishing it with embroidery.

▲ OCEAN WAVES, 48" x 48", 1993, BY THE AUTHOR.

▲ STARFIRE (DETAIL OF BACK), 1993, BY THE AUTHOR.

▲ SANTA MARIA (DETAIL OF BACK), 1992, BY VELMA McCABE, HANFORD, CALIFORNIA.

Chapter Five
Patterns

If you have never sewn any kind of a round design before, start with simple designs and work up to the ones with more complicated piecing. Stars with 16 points are half the amount of work as those with 32 points, just because there are half as many pieces. The 12-point rainbow colored star would be a good block to practice with because it is fairly simple.

The patterns given here are as precise as I can make them and you need to make your work as precise as you can manage. If you photocopy the pages to make templates, check to see that the photocopy machine has not distorted the shapes. Compare the copy to the original by holding them up to the light and lining up the shapes. I have found that when I try to reduce or enlarge with a photocopy machine there is often distortion. When following a line, always cut or stitch directly down the *middle* of the line to insure accuracy.

The patterns are given in a variety of ways. Several of the pieced stars include seam allowances and can be easily used with traditional piecing methods. There are also several patterns given without seam allowances because they work well with the freezer paper template method. Any of the patterns can be adapted to either method by adding or eliminating seam allowances from the patterns. You can also create paper foundation templates from any of the patterns by nesting the pattern shapes together and making a new, single template for each pieceable segment. Appliqué patterns are given without seam allowances.

All of the patterns are given as circles and some include patterns for a background block. If the pattern is too large to include a background block pattern go to page 95 for information on how to create a background block.

PATTERN 1

Double Rainbow Star
12 Points

11" diameter with a 12" block

I originally designed this pattern to use in a watch face because it has twelve points on the outside but the center star clearly defines 1, 3, 6 and 9. It made an easy-to-read watch design.

This is a good pattern for you to start with if you have never sewn a radiating star before. It has a minimum of points and only a few pattern shapes. Use the center star as a practice for learning paper foundation piecing or eliminate the star and use a large center circle.

The center star is given as a full size paper foundation cut into four segments. See Construction Chapter 4 and follow the diagrams on page 60.

The pattern for the outer star is offered with seam allowances for traditional piecing methods.

The diagram shows the back side of the design. The finished star will be reversed.

▲ DOUBLE RAINBOW BLOCK, 12" UNQUILTED BLOCK, 1992, BY THE AUTHOR.

Cut two strips of contrasting fabric, each 1¹/₄" x 12" for piece #1.

Cut two strips of similar fabric, each 2" x 8" for piece #2; or cut one strip 2" x 16" for piece #2.

PAPER FOUNDATION METHOD - STAR CENTER

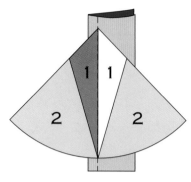

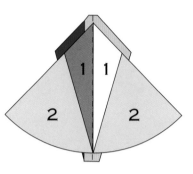

STEP 1. POSITION FABRIC ON BACK OF PAPER PATTERN AND STITCH.

STEP 2. PRESS SEAM AND TRIM.

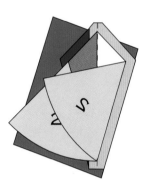

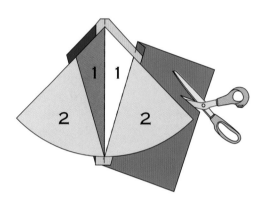

STEP 3. POSITION ON NEXT FABRIC.

STEP 4. STITCH. PRESS SEAM AND TRIM.

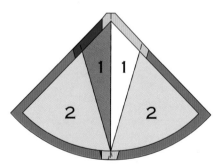

STEP 5. REPEAT ON OPPOSITE SIDE WITH SECOND #2 PIECE. SEW FOUR OF THESE SECTIONS TOGETHER TO COMPLETE THE STAR. PRESS SEAMS OPEN.

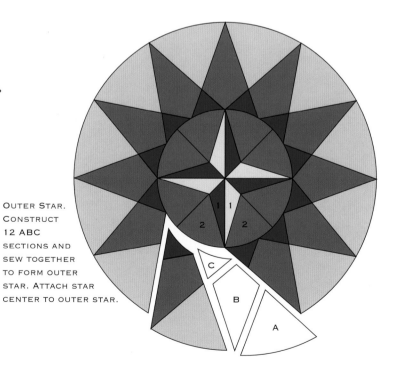

OUTER STAR. CONSTRUCT 12 ABC SECTIONS AND SEW TOGETHER TO FORM OUTER STAR. ATTACH STAR CENTER TO OUTER STAR.

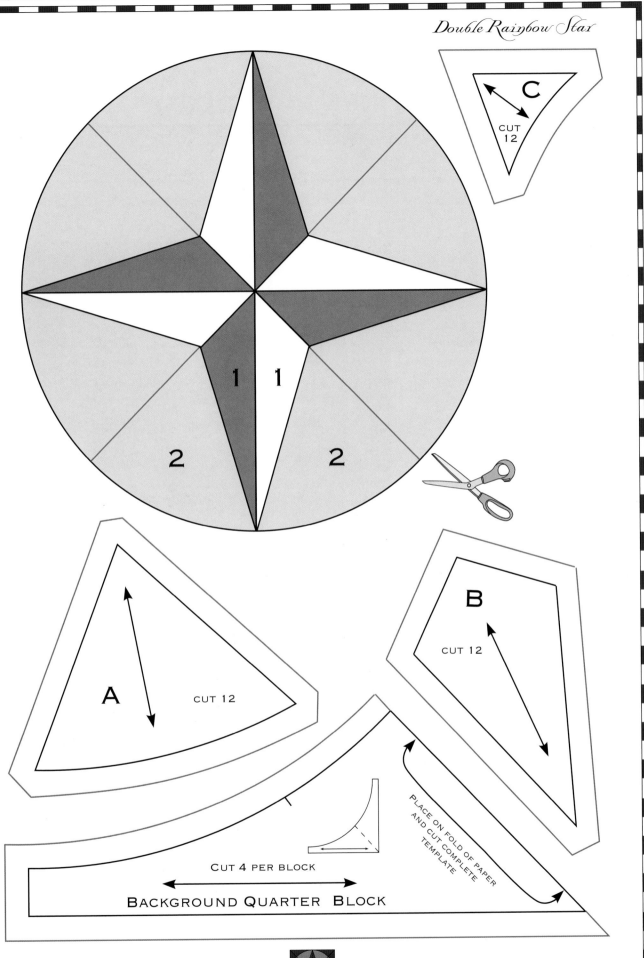

C
CUT
12

1 1

2   2

B
CUT 12

A   CUT 12

PLACE ON FOLD OF PAPER
AND CUT COMPLETE
TEMPLATE

CUT 4 PER BLOCK

BACKGROUND QUARTER BLOCK

PATTERN 2

Mariner's Compass
16 Points with 32-Point option

15" diameter with a 16", 17", or 18" block

Shirley Sydow has used her collection of plaids and stripes to make this wonderful quilt.

The pattern is offered for the freezer paper template method, efficiently nested together so that you can cut all the pieces by stacking four sheets of freezer paper together and cutting them at one time. Make a photocopy of the pattern or trace onto freezer paper. Stack the patterns so that you will have four sheets of freezer paper (dull side to shiny side). Tack the sheets of freezer paper together with the tip of an iron at the X marks. Cut through all the layers accurately with scissors or a rotary cutter.

See the Freezer Paper Template section of the Construction chapter for more instructions, page 44. If you would like to make a 32-point star, see the combination methods section on page 51. The pattern is indicated by the dashed line on piece A.

▲ Starring Plaids, 84" x 91", 1994, by Shirley Sydow, West Hills, California.

▲ Starring Plaids (detail).

Sunburst variation — *cut 16 A's, 8 B's, 4 C's and 4 C/D's*

Starflower variation — *cut 16 A's, 8 B's, 8 C's and 8 D's*

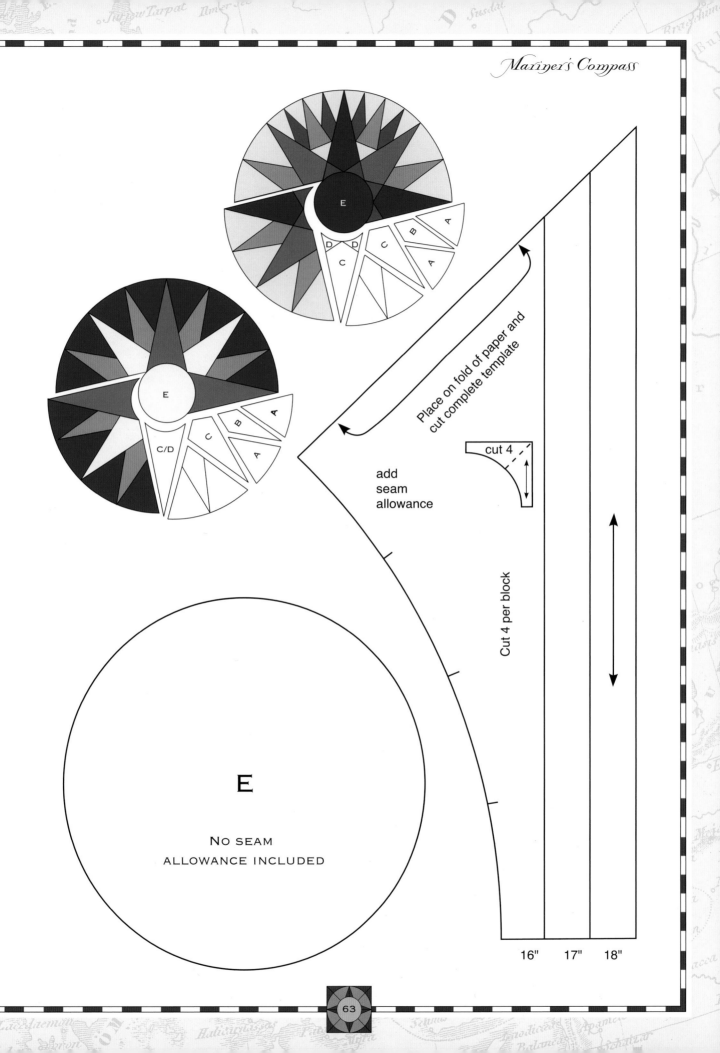

Place on fold of paper and
cut complete template

cut 4

add
seam
allowance

Cut 4 per block

E

No seam
allowance included

16"   17"   18"

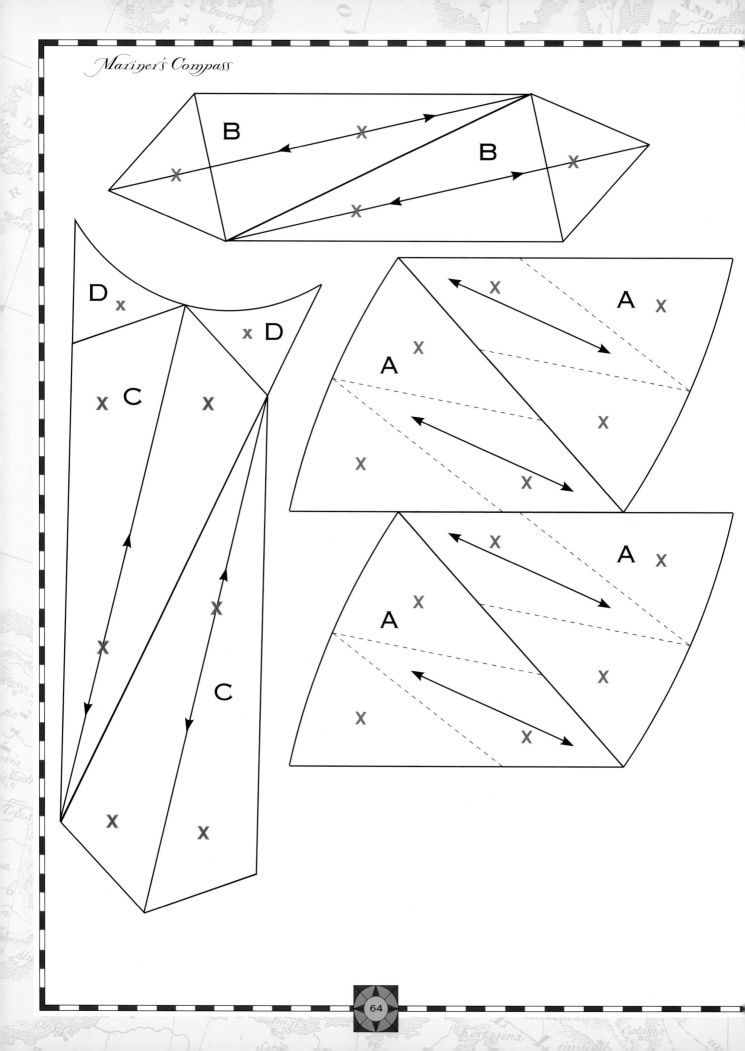

Plaid Mariner's Compass
32 Points

18" diameter with a 20" block

▲ PLAID MARINER'S COMPASS, 96" X 96", 1989, BY THE AUTHOR.

PLAID MARINER'S COMPASS
(DETAIL).

This large traditional block was used in the bed quilt shown at the left. I wanted to make something that reminded me of several antique quilts I had seen but couldn't afford to purchase. Plaid and stripe fabrics were used to make the stars. Cut-out, printed flowers were appliquéd in the centers of the blocks.

The pattern given includes seam allowances for the traditional piecing method. The split ray (B), can be pieced first or the whole ray can be cut from pre-sewn fabric. The 4½" Star pattern given in Chapter Four can be used in the center of this star.

BASTING TEMPLATE
NO SEAM ALLOWANCE INCLUDED

F

CUT 1

SEE PAGE 49
FOR THE STAR PATTERN

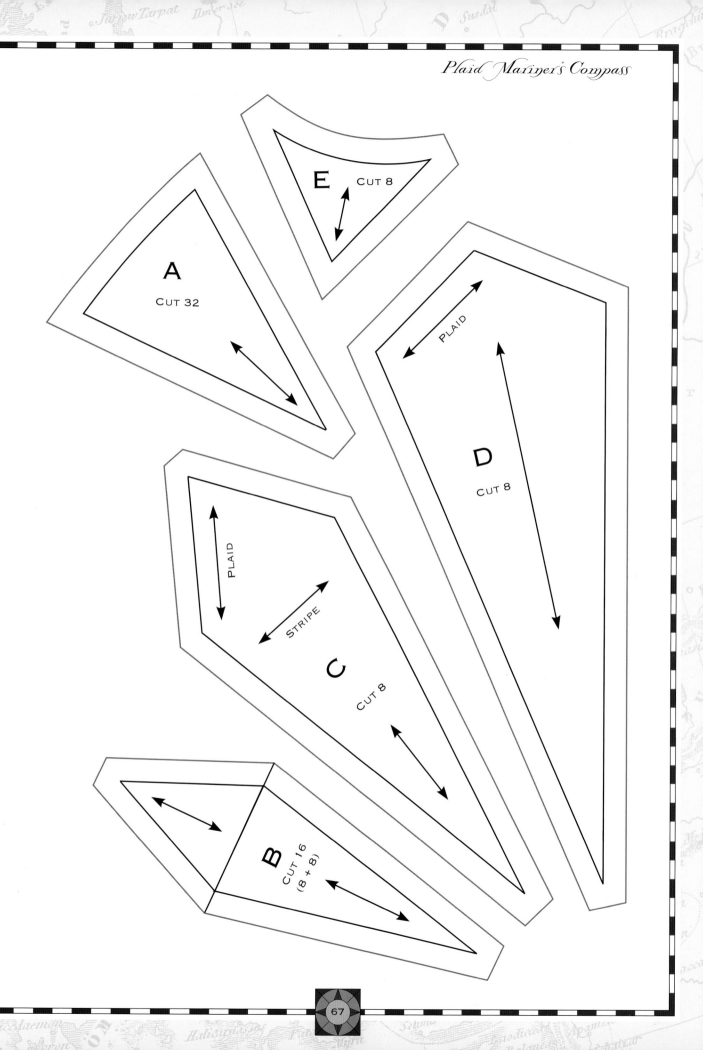

Split Star
16 Points

15" diameter with a 16" block

This star can be converted to segments and sewn using the paper foundation method. Photocopy or trace the pattern onto paper four times, then cut apart into eight segments. A slick trick is to stack four pieces of paper (freezer or thin paper) with the pattern and make copies by sewing through the lines with an empty needle on the sewing machine.

See the Paper Foundation section in the Construction chapter. Cut strips of fabric for each piece the width given. Be sure to shorten your stitch length.

▲ SPLIT STAR,
33" x 33", 1994,
BY THE AUTHOR.

Cut two strips of contrasting fabric, each $1^1/_2$" by approximately 44" long for piece #1.

Cut strips $3^1/_2$" by approximately 72" long for pieces #2 and #3.

Cut two strips of contrasting fabric, each $1^3/_4$" by approximately 26" long for piece #4.

Cut two strips of contrasting fabric, each $2^1/_4$" by approximately 34" long for piece #5.

CUT HERE

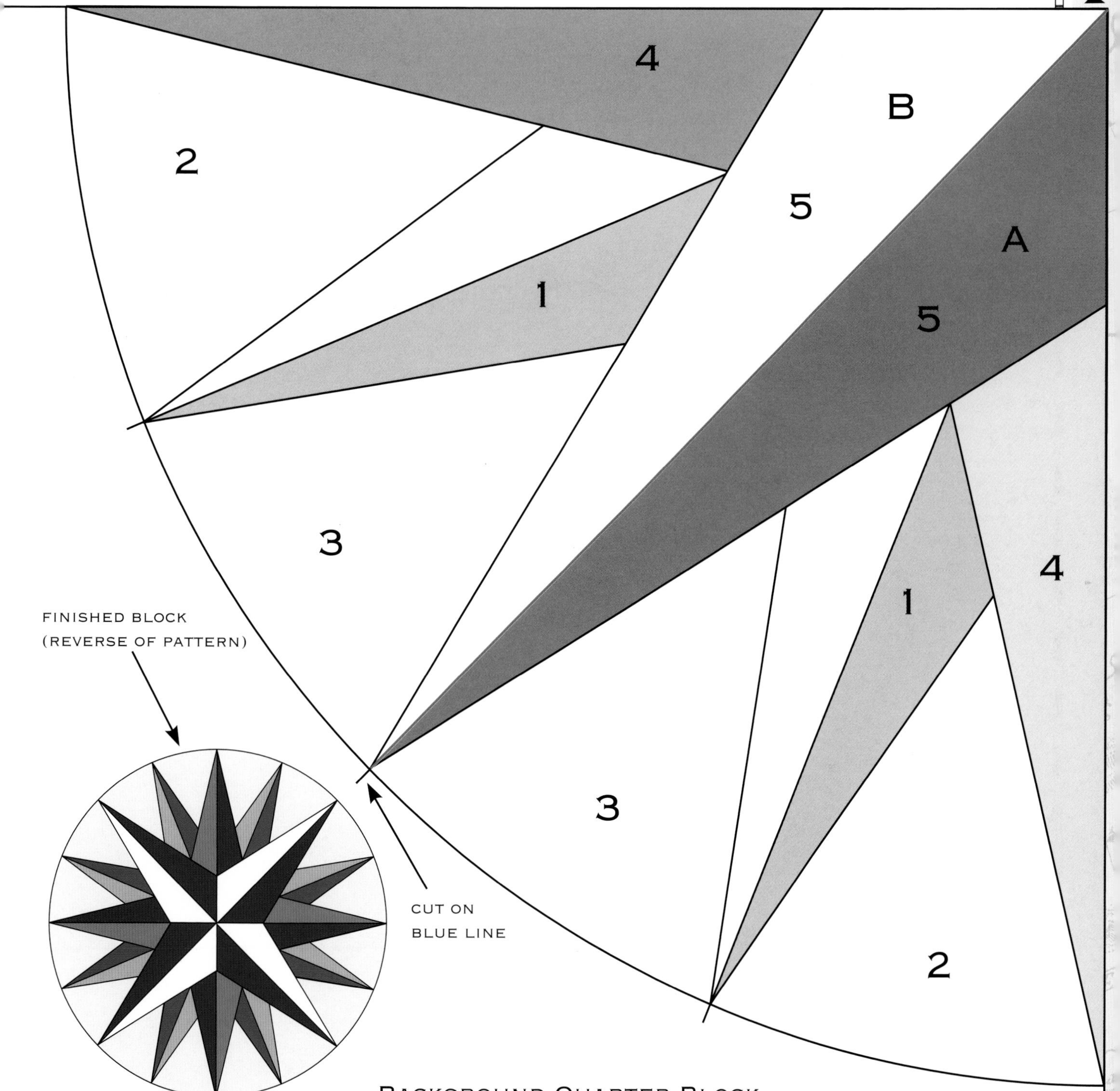

4

B

2

5

1

A

5

3

FINISHED BLOCK
(REVERSE OF PATTERN)

1

4

3

CUT ON
BLUE LINE

2

BACKGROUND QUARTER BLOCK

SPLIT STAR FOR PAPER PIECING - 15" DIAMETER.

Mariner's Compass

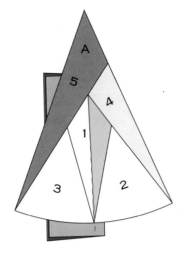

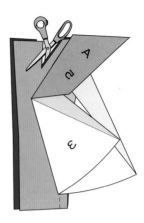

STEP 1. PLACE STRIPS RIGHT SIDES TOGETHER WITH THE LIGHT STRIP ON TOP. FOLD PATTERN AND POSITION ON TOP OF THE FABRIC STRIPS FOR PIECE #1.

STEP 2. STITCH THROUGH PAPER AND FABRIC TO THE INTERSECTING POINT.

STEP 3. FOLD AND TRIM.

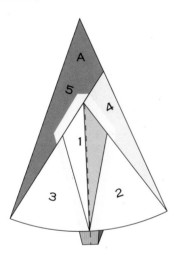

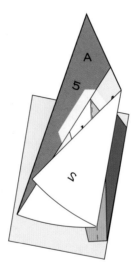

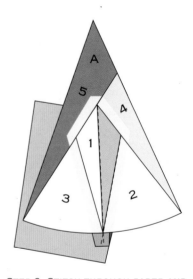

STEP 4. PRESS.

STEP 5. FOLD PATTERN AND POSITION ON TOP OF THE FABRIC FOR PIECE #2.

STEP 6. STITCH THROUGH PAPER AND FABRIC TO THE INTERSECTING POINT.

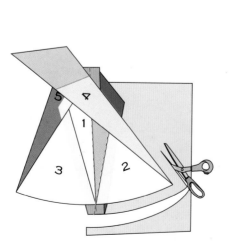

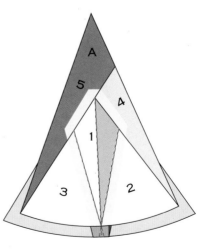

STEP 7. PRESS AND TRIM.

STEP 8. REPEAT FOR PIECE #3 ON OPPOSITE SIDE.

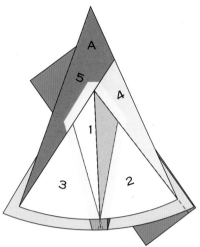

STEP 9. REPEAT FOR PIECE #4. POSITION THE FABRIC STRIP FOR #4 UNDERNEATH, WITH RIGHT SIDES OF THE FABRIC FACING AND STITCH.

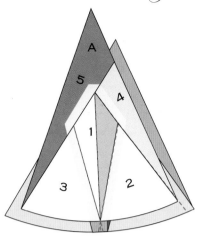

STEP 10. PRESS AND TRIM.

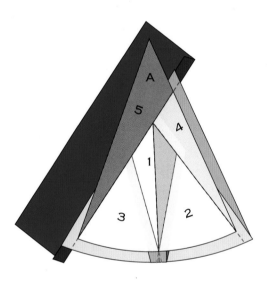

STEP 11. REPEAT FOR #5. POSITON, STITCH, PRESS.

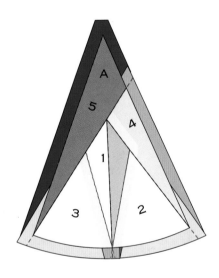

STEP 12. TRIM.

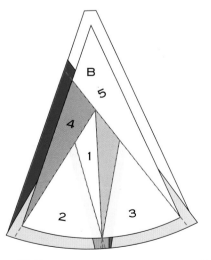

STEP 13. REPEAT WITH OPPOSITE SEGMENT B.

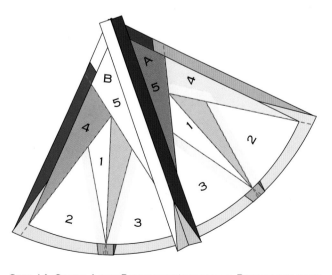

STEP 14. STITCH A AND B SEGMENTS TOGETHER. PRESS SEAM OPEN. STITCH FOUR A/B SEGMENTS TOGETHER TO COMPLETE THE STAR.

New York Beauty Block

7" block with three variations

Using the paper foundation method makes this intimidating looking design much easier to sew than using traditional methods. The paper stabilizes the small points while you sew them. A traditional New York Beauty is pictured on page 21. and two contemporary variations, *Florida Doo Dah Day* on page 20 and *New York Beauty* appear on page 21. If the pattern isn't the right size, enlarge or reduce it using a photocopy machine, but be sure to use a copy machine that will not distort the pattern.

Make a paper copy of the pattern for each unit you plan to make. If you make photocopies be sure they are from the same original and check for distortion. Cut the pattern apart on the line of the segments you will need. Remember to change the stitch length of your sewing machine to 20 stitches to the inch. Seam allowances must be added to the pattern when you cut the fabric and be sure to trace the matching marks so that you can piece the curves accurately into each other. See Chapter Four for more information on paper foundation piecing methods.

Cut one strip for B dark triangles $1^{1}/_{2}$" by approximately 25" long.

Cut one strip for B light triangles $1^{3}/_{4}$" by approximately 25" long.

Cut one strip for D dark triangles $1^{1}/_{2}$" by approximately 9" long.

Cut one strip for D light triangles $1^{3}/_{4}$" by approximately 10" long.

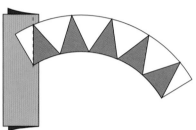

STEP 1. PLACE A LIGHT AND DARK STRIP TOGETHER WITH RIGHT SIDES FACING AND THE LIGHT STRIP ON TOP. POSITION THE PAPER PATTERN, ON TOP OF THE FABRICS, WITH THE RAW FABRIC EDGE EXTENDING $^{1}/_{4}$" TO THE RIGHT OF THE LINE YOU WILL BE STITCHING. STITCH.

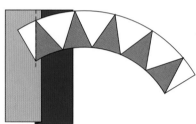

STEP 2. PRESS.

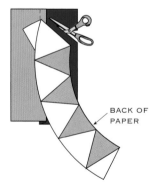

BACK OF PAPER

STEP 3. FOLD THE PAPER BACK AND TRIM THE SEAM ALLOWANCE.

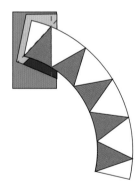

STEP 4. TRIM OFF THE EXTRA FABRIC STRIP. PLACE A LIGHT STRIP UNDER THE DARK STRIP WITH THE RIGHT SIDE UP AND THE EDGE EXTENDING $^{1}/_{4}$" PAST THE LINE YOU WILL BE STITCHING. STITCH, PRESS AND TRIM. CONTINUE.

STEP 5. REPEAT TO COMPLETE D AND B ARCS.

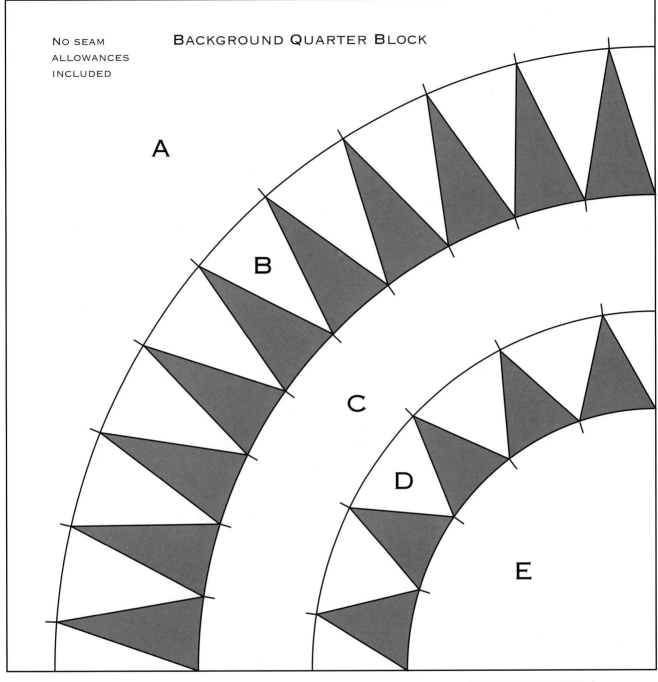

BACKGROUND QUARTER BLOCK

NO SEAM ALLOWANCES INCLUDED

A

B

C

D

E

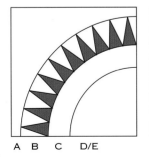

A B C D/E

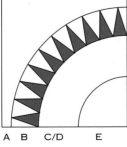

A B C/D E

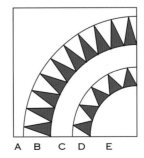

A B C D E

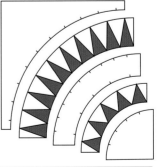

VARIATIONS

STEP 6. PIECE THE SEGMENTS TOGETHER WITH THE
REMAINING CURVED SECTIONS OF THE DESIGN USING THE
CONFIGURATION SHOWN ABOVE.

PATTERN 6

Fleur-de-lis Patterns

▲ BRODERIE PERSE MARINER'S COMPASS, 45" X 45", 1991, BY THE AUTHOR.

1. Needleturn method.

Make a template (without seam allowances) and draw around it on the *front* side of the fabric. Cut out the fabric leaving a scant ¼" seam allowance. Position and baste it on the quilt block. Use the needle to turn under the seam allowance as you appliqué with small stitches using matching thread. Finger press as you go. You will need to clip the inward points.

2. Spray starch method.

Make a template (without seam allowances) from file folder or other coated cardboard. Draw around the template on the *back* of the fabric and cut out the fabric leaving a scant ¼" seam allowance. Clip inner curves almost up to the seam line.

Spray some starch into a shallow bowl. Use your fingers or a small brush to dab some liquid starch onto the seam allowances of the fleur-de-lis fabric. Lay the template on the back of the fabric and use the tip of the iron to press the wet fabric around the coated cardboard template. When the fabric is ironed dry, unstick the seam allowances from the cardboard with a pin. Remove the template. Position the fleur-de-lis on the quilt block and appliqué with small stitches using matching thread.

I love the fleur-de-lis design and have included four different variations. A study of old maps or books about cartography will probably give you even more ideas. You can use a photocopy machine to enlarge or reduce the patterns to fit your designs.

The fleur-de-lis designs can be cut from just one fabric although cartographers often show them with dark and light sides and split center points. Cut apart the pattern pieces to make templates.

After appliquéing in place, apply the center bar joining the pieces.

You can position the design at the top of the northern point as well as within it or even replace it. See pages 68 and 74. While it is customary on maps to have north at the top, you can position it wherever you wish. See page 76.

While I don't want to get into a whole chapter on how to appliqué, I will suggest two methods which work well for me on these patterns.

PATTERN 7

Sunflowers
12 Points

6" diameter with an 8" block
8" diameter with a 10" block
10" diameter with a 12" block

▲ JUST SUNFLOWERS, 44" x 44", 1993, BY THE AUTHOR.

Mariner's Compass

The traditional Sunflower block is related to the Mariner's Compass, but it is slightly harder to sew because of the abrupt turn at the intersection of triangles C and A. It is offered here in three sizes with 12 points. I used it in several sizes with lots of sunflower print fabrics in the contemporary wallhanging on page 77.

The antique quilt Virginia Sunflower, detail on page 9, shows a block with 13 points.

The patterns include seam allowances for the traditional piecing method. Remember to add a ¼" seam allowance to the center (D) and to the background quarter blocks. The matching marks on the background quarter block match the points of the star.

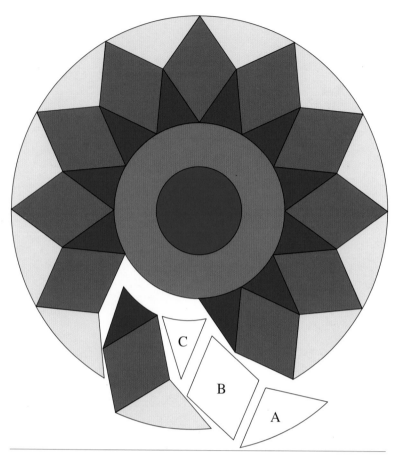

Cut 12 each of pieces A, B and C.

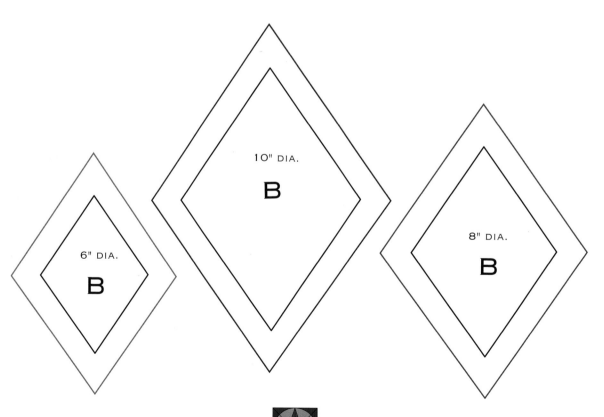

10" DIA.

B

6" DIA.

B

8" DIA.

B

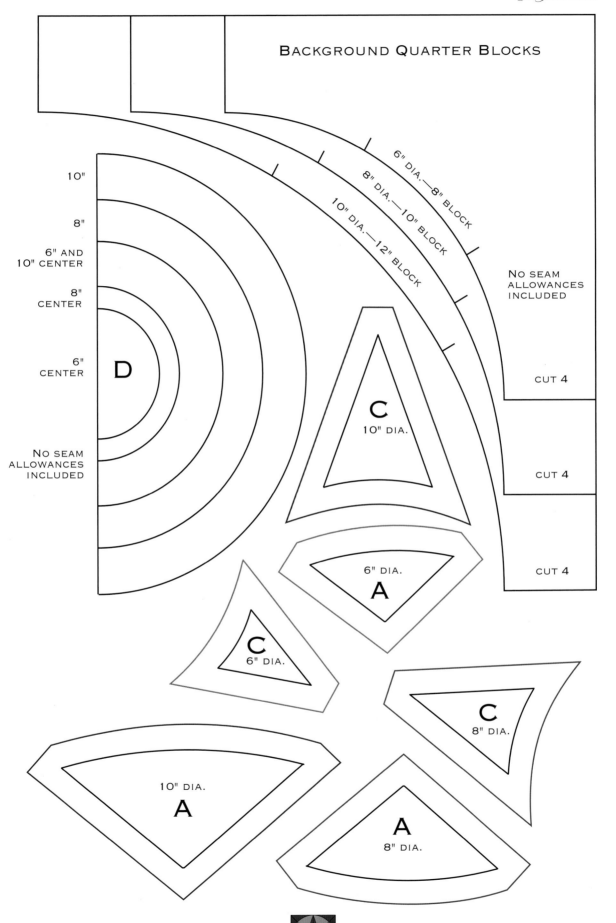

BACKGROUND QUARTER BLOCKS

6" DIA.—8" BLOCK

8" DIA.—10" BLOCK

10" DIA.—12" BLOCK

NO SEAM
ALLOWANCES
INCLUDED

CUT 4

CUT 4

CUT 4

10"

8"

6" AND
10" CENTER

8"
CENTER

6"
CENTER

D

NO SEAM
ALLOWANCES
INCLUDED

C
10" DIA.

A
6" DIA.

C
6" DIA.

C
8" DIA.

A
10" DIA.

A
8" DIA.

PATTERN 8

Cartwheel Costa Rica
18 Points

30" diameter with a 12" diameter center

▲ CARTWHEEL COSTA RICA, 43" X 43", 1994, BY THE AUTHOR.

This pattern is based on the folk art designs of the farmers of Costa Rica. They paint the huge mahogany wheels of their ox-carts as well as the carts themselves. This particular design was taken from a tourist souvenir painting given to me by the Rev. and Mrs. L.M. McCoy of Decatur, GA. shown on page 7.

The patterns are offered nested together for paper foundation piecing, but they can be cut apart for the freezer paper template method. You can also add seam allowances and use traditional piecing methods. The diagrams and patterns show the back side of the design. The finished star will be reversed.

Strips of fabric can be sewn together to create the dark/light points and then cut pieces B through E using these pre-sewn fabrics. Iron the seam allowance open and then iron the freezer paper templates to the back of the pre-sewn fabrics or mark using traditional templates.

For the inner star, use the marks on G/H to match to the marks on I. Work in one direction, matching the 1 & 2 on the left side with the point of the ray and the 2 on the right side on the next piece. The extra fabric on piece G/H allows for the size of the inner star circle to be adjusted when seaming it to the outer star.

If you use traditional template methods be sure to mark all of the patterns for both of the stars on the same side of the fabric, as the design is not reversible.

The outer star and the inner star are pieced together. The center (I) of the star is appliquéd.

See page 95 for instructions on how to draft the background piece.

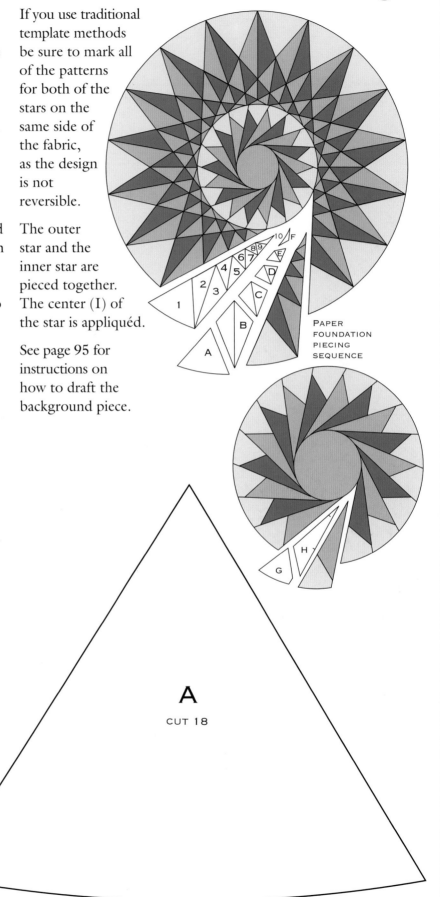

PAPER
FOUNDATION
PIECING
SEQUENCE

A

CUT 18

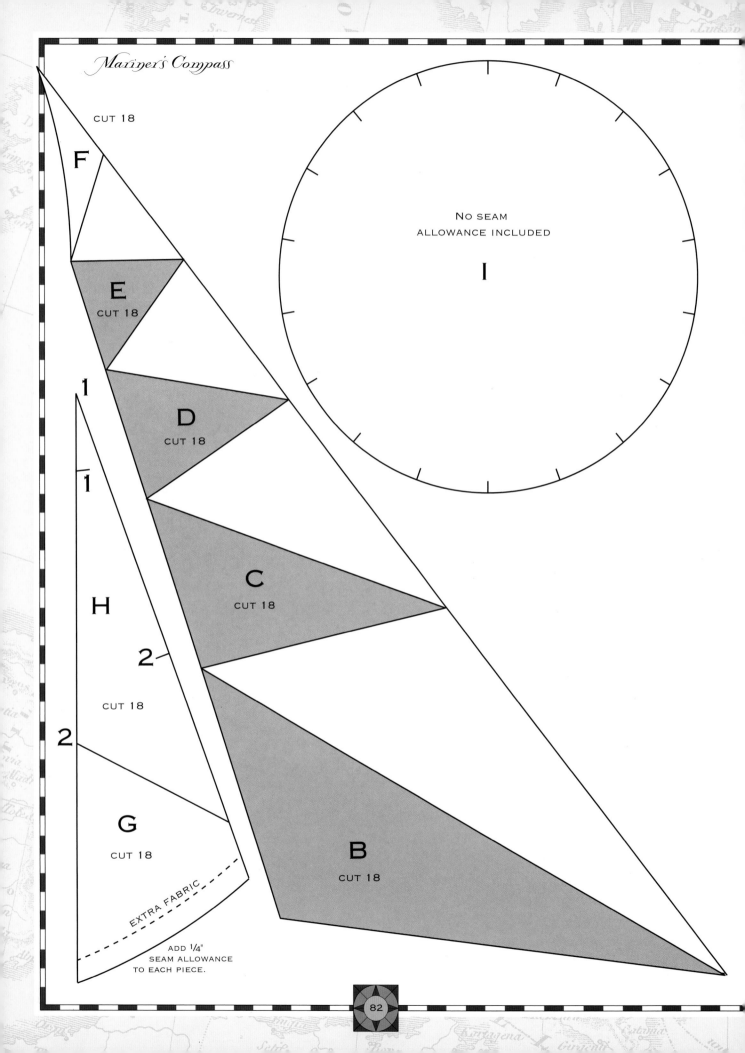

Mariner's Compass

CUT 18

F

E
CUT 18

1

D
CUT 18

1

H
CUT 18

1

2

2

C
CUT 18

G
CUT 18

2

EXTRA FABRIC

ADD ¼"
SEAM ALLOWANCE
TO EACH PIECE.

B
CUT 18

NO SEAM
ALLOWANCE INCLUDED

I

Starfire
16 Points

25" diameter outer star with an 11" diameter inner star

The *Starfire* quilt was inspired by a crazy quilt made by Susan McCord in Indiana in 1895. While she probably thought of her pattern as a fan, she did set the blocks together so that the fans created whole circles. As you examine the photograph of *Starfire* (see page 18) notice that the blocks are actually quarter-circle fans set into the opposite corners of a square.

Space does not allow me to offer detailed instructions on how to assemble the complete *Starfire* quilt. However I have included the two pattern pieces (J and K) which can be used to make the blocks with two quarter-circle fans. I used strip-piecing of the paper foundations to create the background. Also included are the schematics to allow you to arrange those blocks the way I did in *Starfire*. During the design process for the quilt we came up with lots of different possibilities for combining the stars and fans. You could try to play around and come up with new combinations yourself.

▲ STARFIRE (DETAIL), 1993, BY THE AUTHOR.

The patterns are offered as freezer paper templates with two variations for both the inner and outer star. Pre-sew strips of dark and light fabric together, press the seams open and iron the freezer paper templates on the back. See Chapter Four page 44 for more information about freezer paper templates.

You can add seam allowances to the pattern for the traditional template methods or nest the patterns together to make segments of eight to use with the paper foundation method.

Diagrams and patterns show the back side of the design. The finished star will be reversed.

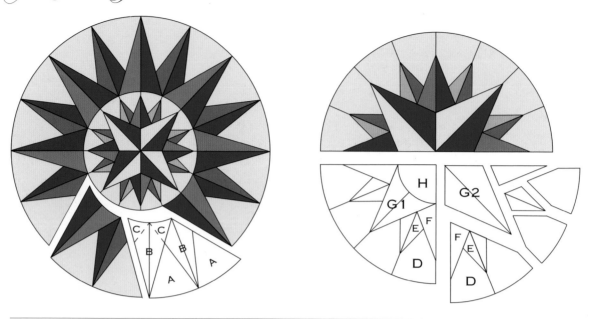

THE BLOCKS ARE PIECED AS SHOWN.

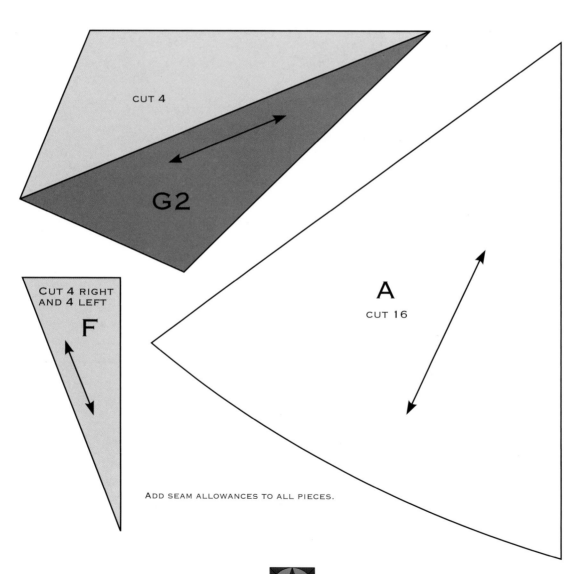

CUT 4

G2

CUT 4 RIGHT
AND 4 LEFT

F

A

CUT 16

ADD SEAM ALLOWANCES TO ALL PIECES.

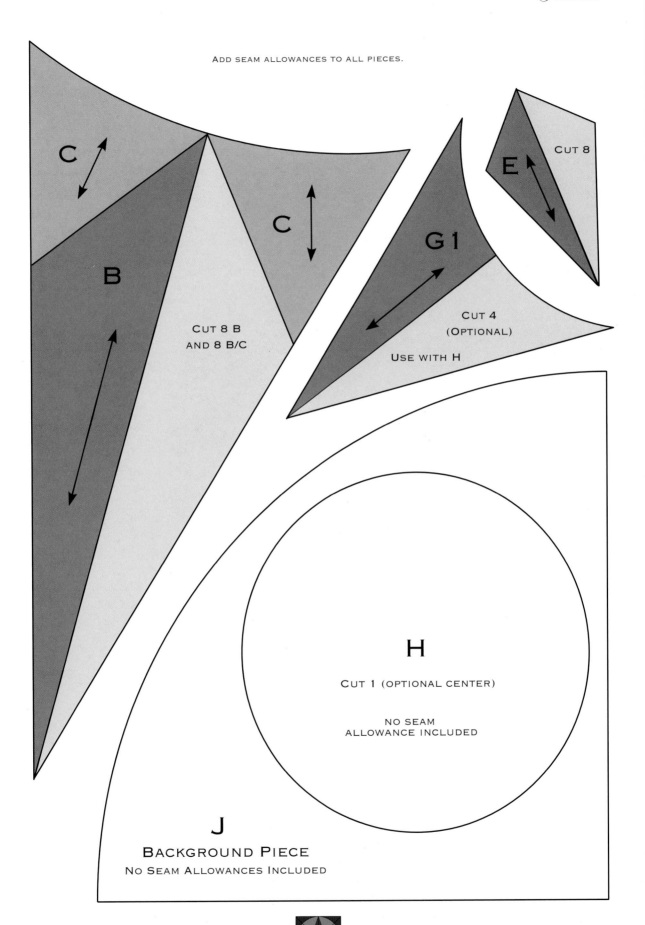

ADD SEAM ALLOWANCES TO ALL PIECES.

Starfire

C

C

B

CUT 8 B
AND 8 B/C

E

CUT 8

G1

CUT 4
(OPTIONAL)

USE WITH H

H

CUT 1 (OPTIONAL CENTER)

NO SEAM
ALLOWANCE INCLUDED

J

BACKGROUND PIECE
NO SEAM ALLOWANCES INCLUDED

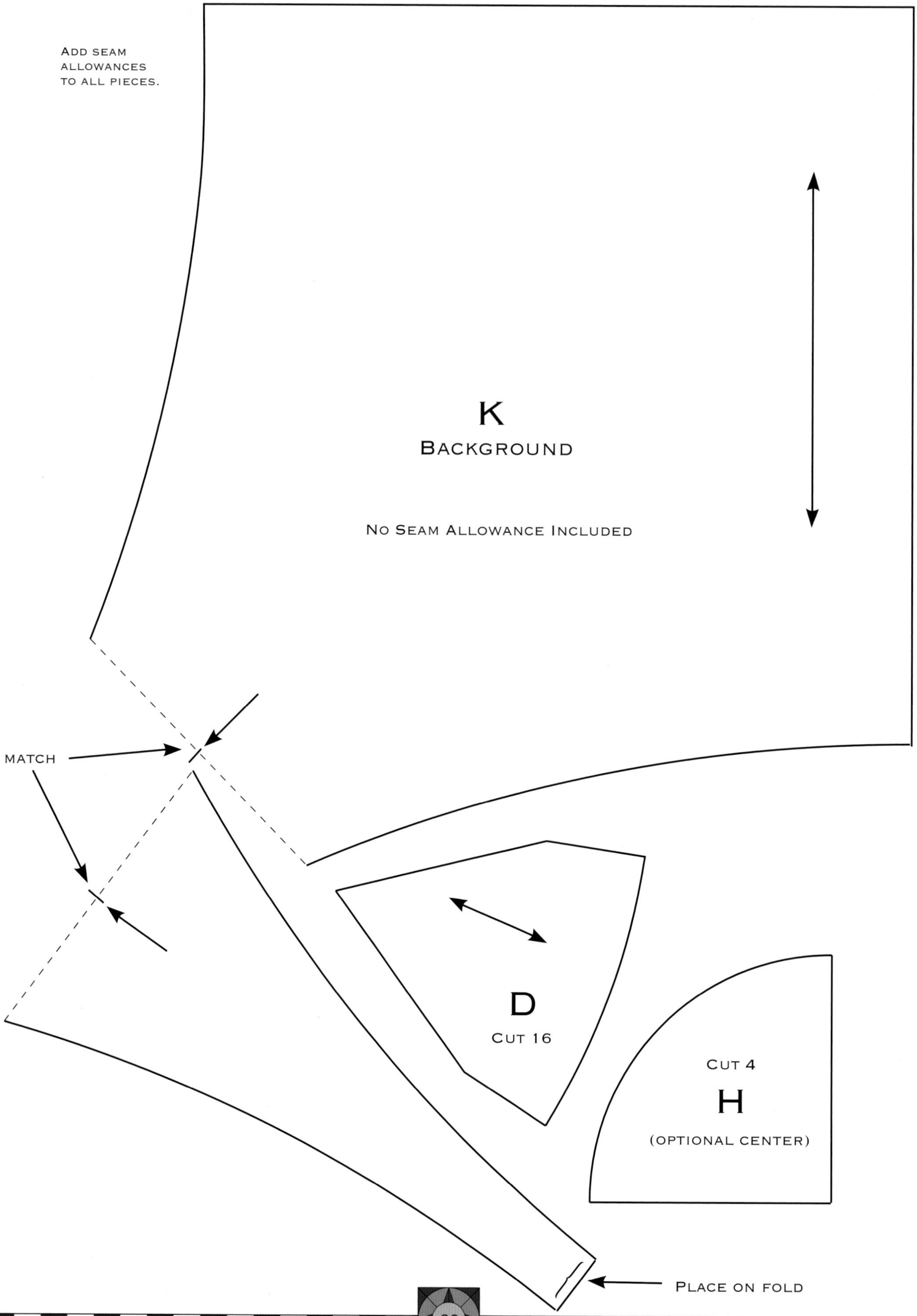

ADD SEAM
ALLOWANCES
TO ALL PIECES.

K
BACKGROUND

NO SEAM ALLOWANCE INCLUDED

MATCH

D
CUT 16

CUT 4
H
(OPTIONAL CENTER)

PLACE ON FOLD

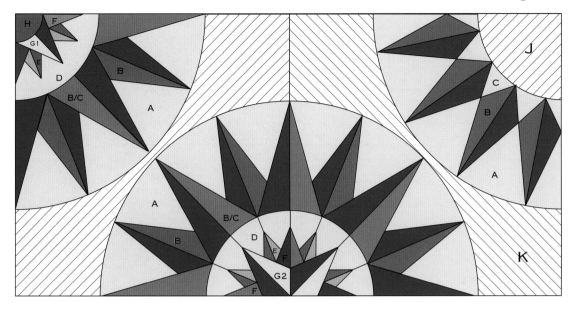

LAYOUT OF THE QUILT ON THE COVER.

PATTERN 10

Twilight Star
20 Points

24" and 36" diameter

This 20-point star is one of my favorites. It was offered in the 30" size in my previous book, and all of the examples shown in this book are made using this size pattern: *Madras Star* on page 35, *Cut-off Star* on page 89 and *Night Lights* on page 14. It is offered in two new sizes because it has proved so versatile and so many people have requested even larger stars. It is a simplified version of the large center star from *Nautical Stars* on page 36. The fabrics used in the largest ray (B) could be strip-pieced before cutting as seen in *Night Lights*.

The pattern for the outer star is offered with seam allowances for traditional piecing methods. If you prefer using freezer paper templates, remove all the seam allowances and cut a paper pattern for each piece. See Chapter Four page 44 for more information. The paper foundation method can also be used by nesting all of the pattern pieces together without seam allowances to create a large paper wedge.

▲ TWILIGHT STAR,
35" X 35", 1993,
BY THE AUTHOR.

The inner star patterns are offered as paper foundation patterns. See Chapter Four page 48 for more information. If you prefer to use template methods cut the pattern apart.

See page 95 for information on how to draft background blocks.

▲ CUT-OFF STAR, 30" X 30", BY THE AUTHOR.

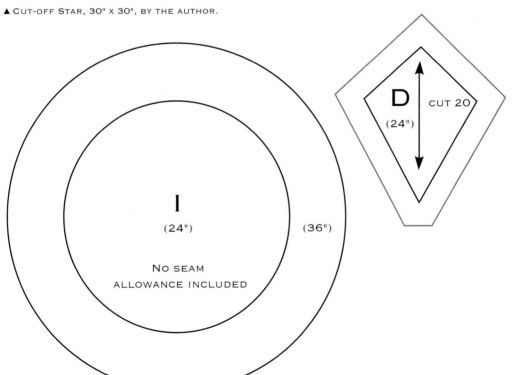

I
(24")

(36")

NO SEAM
ALLOWANCE INCLUDED

D
(24")

CUT 20

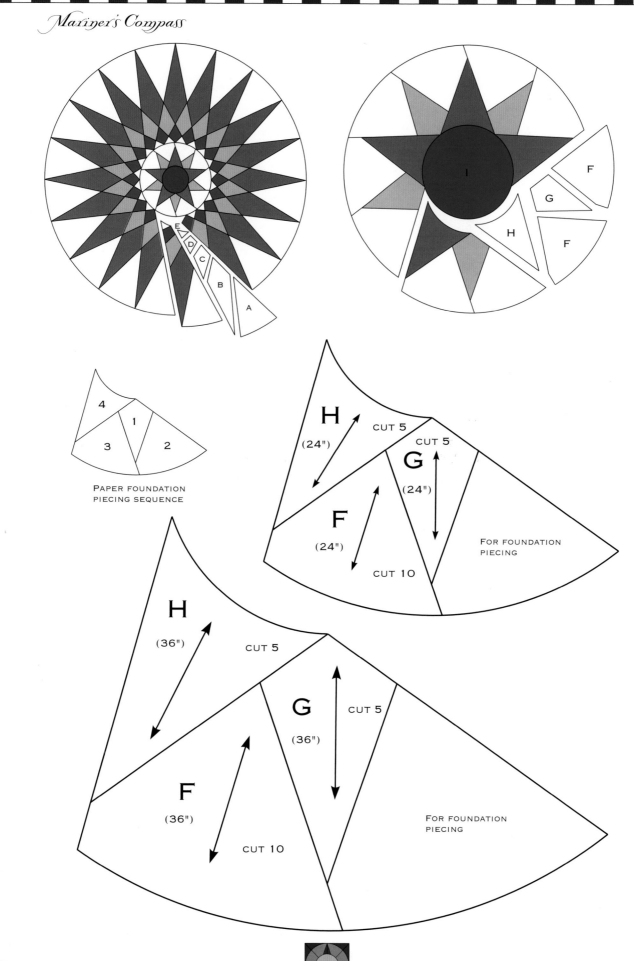

Mariner's Compass

PAPER FOUNDATION
PIECING SEQUENCE

H
(24")
CUT 5

G
(24")
CUT 5

F
(24")
CUT 10

FOR FOUNDATION
PIECING

H
(36")
CUT 5

G
(36")
CUT 5

F
(36")
CUT 10

FOR FOUNDATION
PIECING

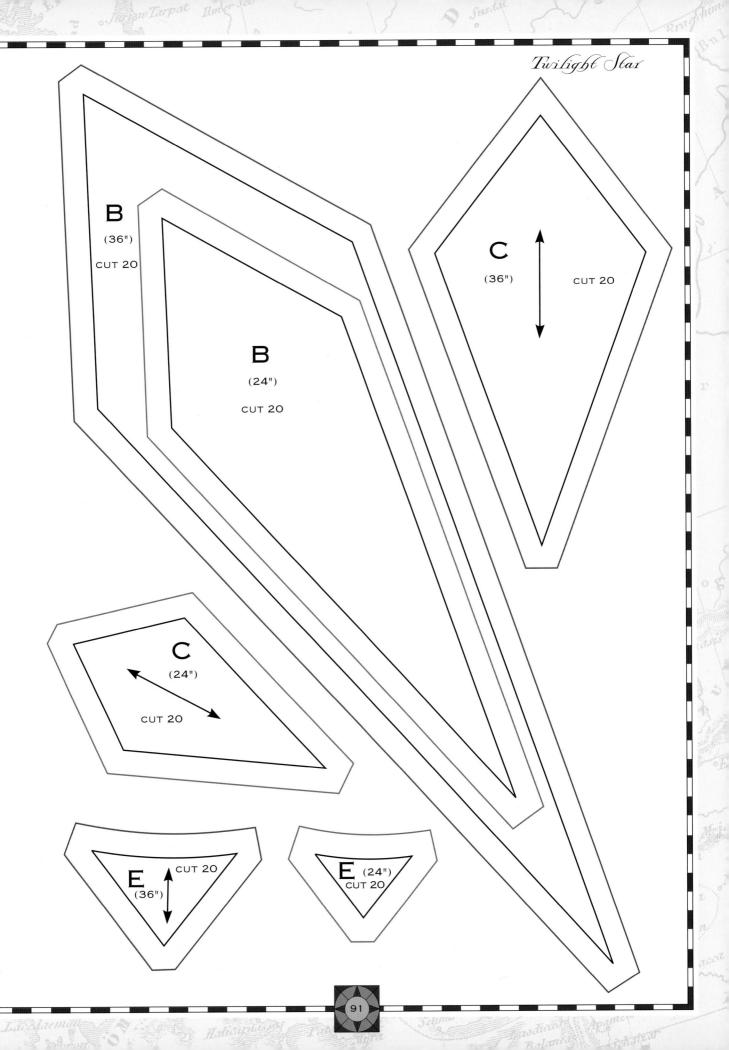

B
(36")
CUT 20

B
(24")
CUT 20

C
(36")
CUT 20

C
(24")
CUT 20

E
(36")
CUT 20

E (24")
CUT 20

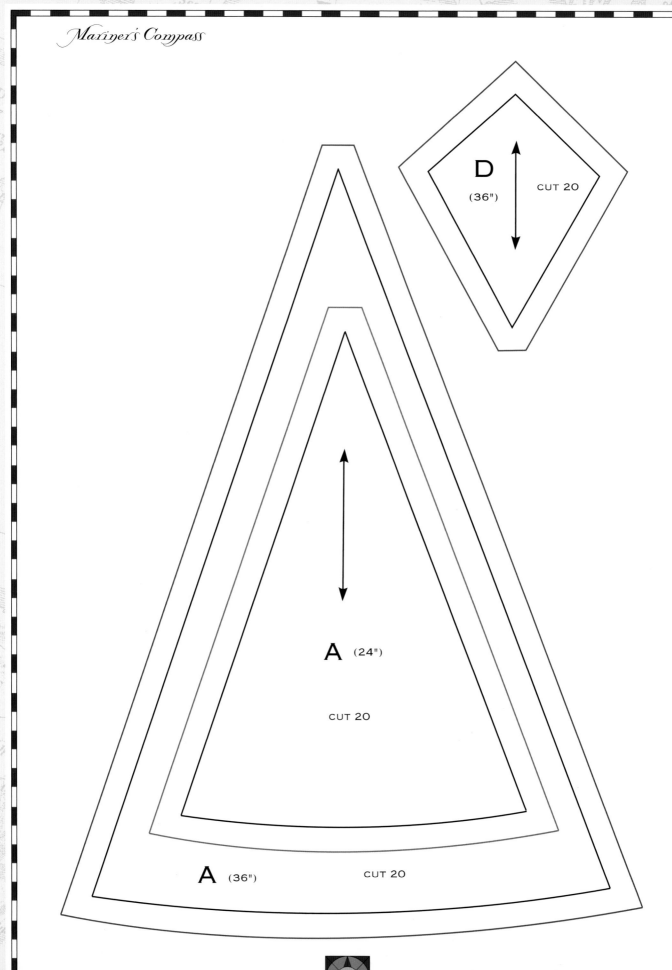

D
(36")
CUT 20

A (24")

CUT 20

A (36")   CUT 20

Off-Center Star
16 Points

17" diameter with an 18" block. See pullout section in back of book.

Several variations are offered. Trace the full size pattern onto the dull side of freezer paper. Be sure to include the correct number, letter and matching marks for each piece in the variation you plan to make. See the Freezer Paper Template section of the Construction chapter, page 44 for more instructions.

Diagrams are shown for the back side of the design. Finished stars will be reversed.

▲ NORTHERN STARS,
63" x 73", 1993,
BY THE AUTHOR.

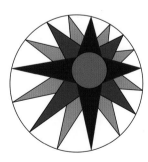

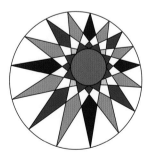

SUNBURST   STARFLOWER I   STARFLOWER II   CONCENTRIC

PATTERNS 12 AND 13

Oval Star
16 Points

17" x 26" with an 18" x 27" block. See pullout section at back of book.

The patterns are offered as one quarter of the full size design in two variations: Oval with round center and Oval with oval center. Use the freezer paper method to avoid the confusion caused by the number of different shapes and the need for reversals.

Trace the full size quadrant onto the dull side of the freezer paper. Make two copies as shown and two in reverse (turn the pattern over and trace the back side of the pattern). Give each piece in each quadrant a different number if you are using the freezer paper template method. Split ray variations can be made with paper foundation methods by breaking the design into pieceable segments. See page 48. You can use combination methods shown on page 51 for adding an extra set of rays between the 16 points.

▲ PURPLE OVAL STAR, 29" x 40", 1994, BY THE AUTHOR.

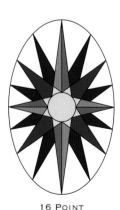

16 POINT

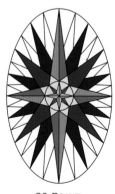

32 POINT

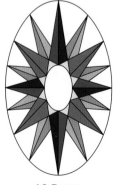

16 POINT

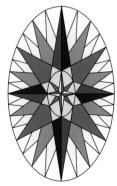

32 POINT

Background Quarter Blocks

Some of the star circles are too large to offer the background pattern. You can draft the pattern yourself using pencil, paper, ruler and perhaps a compass.

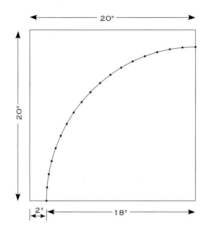

1. Determine the diameter of the star circle. Each pattern has the diameter listed immediately under the title.

   Example: Twilight Star, 36" diameter

2. Decide how big you want the background block to be.

   Example: 40" square

3. Calculate one-quarter of the block and draw a square that size on paper.

   Example: 20" square

4. Use your compass (if it is large enough) or a ruler to mark a circle that is one-half the diameter (radius) of the star circle.

   Example: 18" radius

Make matching marks at the seam line of piecing wedge pattern (A) as illustrated.

Add seam allowances to your pattern and cut four from your background fabric.

Follow the instructions on page 54 to attach the star to the background block.

Patterns which do not include a background block are:

Pattern 3
Plaid Mariner's Compass
18" diameter

Pattern 9
Starfire
25" diameter

Pattern 10
Twilight Star
24" diameter and
36" diameter

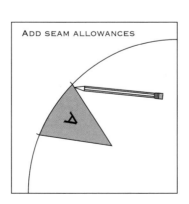

ADD SEAM ALLOWANCES

A

Bibliography

Brackman, Barbara.
New York Beauties.
Quilter's Newsletter Magazine.
January-February 1995, pp. 34-38.
Golden, CO: Leman Publications.

Bryk, Nancy Villa.
Susan McCords's Quilts,
A Farmwife's Legacy.
Dearborn, MI: Publication of the
Henry Ford Museum and
Greenfield Village, 1988.

Fitzgerald, Lisa M.
"Evolution of a Wind Rose."
Sea Frontiers Magazine.
May-June 1990, pp. 44-47.
Publication of The International
Oceanographic Foundation/
University of Miami Rosenstiel
School of Marine and Atmospheric
Science.

Hall, Jane and Haywood, Dixie.
Precision Pieced Quilts Using the
Foundation Method.
Radnor, PA: Chilton Book
Company, 1991.

Mathieson, Judy.
Mariner's Compass:
An American Quilt Classic.
Lafayette, CA: C&T Publishing, 1987.

McCloskey, Marsha.
Lessons in Machine Piecing.
Bothell, WA: That Patchwork
Place, 1990

Shirer, Marie.
"Quiltmaker's Workshop."
Quilter's Newsletter Magazine.
October 1993, pp. 50-51 and 73.
Golden, CO: Leman Publications.

Wells, Jean.
Memorabilia Quilting.
Lafayette, CA: C&T Publishing, 1992

OTHER FINE BOOKS BY C&T PUBLISHING

Appliqué 12 Easy Ways!
Elly Sienkiewicz

The Art of Silk Ribbon Embroidery,
Judith Baker Montano

Beyond the Horizon,
Small Landscape Appliqué,
Valerie Hearder

Buttonhole Stitch Appliqué,
Jean Wells

A Colorful Book,
Yvonne Porcella

Colors Changing Hue,
Yvonne Porcella

Crazy Quilt Handbook,
Judith Montano

Crazy Quilt Odyssey,
Judith Montano

Dating Quilts: From 1600 to the
Present, A Quick and Easy Reference,
Helen Kelley

Elegant Stitches: An Illustrated Stitch
Guide & Source Book of Inspiration,
Judith Baker Montano

The Fabric Makes the Quilt,
Roberta Horton

Faces & Places, Images in Appliqué,
Charlotte Warr Andersen

Heirloom Machine Quilting,
Harriet Hargrave

Imagery on Fabric,
Jean Ray Laury

Impressionist Quilts,
Gai Perry

Isometric Perspective,
Katie Pasquini-Masopust

The Magical Effects of Color,
Joen Wolfrom

Mariner's Compass:
An American Quilt Classic
Judy Mathieson

Mastering Machine Appliqué,
Harriet Hargrave

Nancy Crow:
Improvisational Quilts

Pattern Play,
Doreen Speckmann

Quilts for Fabric Lovers,
Alex Anderson

Quilts, Quilts, and More Quilts!
Diana McClun and Laura Nownes

Schoolhouse Appliqué:
Reverse Techniques and More,
Charlotte Patera

Soft-Edge Piecing,
Jinny Beyer

The Visual Dance: Creating
Spectacular Quilts,
Joen Wolfrom

For more information write for a
free catalog from:

C&T Publishing
P.O. Box 1456
Lafayette, CA 94549
(1-800-284-1114)

W9-BEJ-087

Matter

Matter

ENCOUNTER
THE PHENOMENON

How can you make the best pancakes?

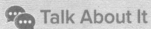

Pancake Transformation

GO ONLINE

Check out *Pancake Transformation* to see the phenomenon in action.

Talk About It

Look at the photo and watch the video of pancakes on an electric griddle. What questions do you have about the phenomenon? Talk about them with a partner.

Did You Know?

Pancakes can be found in almost every culture. The largest pancake ever made was almost 15.24 meters (50 feet) in diameter!

Design the Perfect Pancake

Have you ever wondered how to make the best pancake? You are going to use the skills of a culinary scientists to develop the "best" pancake. By the end of this module, you will identify the criteria and the different materials needed to make the best pancake. Your goal is to design and test the behavior of mixing different materials to make the best pancake.

Lesson 1
Identify Properties of Matter

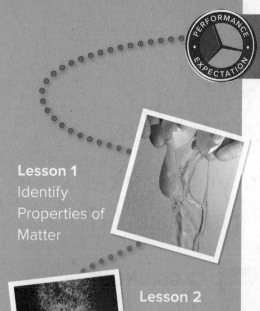

Lesson 2
Mixtures and Solutions

Lesson 3
Physical and Chemical Changes

Lesson 4
Solids, Liquids, and Gases

Culinary scientists apply their knowledge of ingredients to develop new food products that can be produced and sold to consumers in the stores. They perform research, test their ideas, and maintain safety standards so that the new or improved food items can be enjoyed by the public.

 STEM Module Project

Plan and Complete the Engineering Challenge You will use what you learn about matter to design the perfect pancake!

Is it Matter?

Four friends were talking about matter. They each had different ideas about the kinds of things that are matter. This is what they said:

Abe: *I think something needs to be solid to be matter.*

Kayla: *I think matter can be a solid or a liquid.*

Curtis: *I think matter can be a solid, liquid, or gas.*

Lori: *I think matter can be a solid, liquid, or gas, but it doesn't include living things.*

Who do you agree with most? _____

Explain why you agree.

_____

_____

_____

_____

You will revisit the Page Keeley Science Probe later in the lesson.

LESSON 1

Identify Properties of Materials

What are the properties of eggs?

GO ONLINE

Check out *Egg Cracking* to see the phenomenon in action.

Look at the photo and watch the video of an egg cracking. Think about ways that you have seen eggs being used. What questions do you have?

_____

_____

_____

_____

_____

_____

_____

_____

_____

Did You Know?

The average hen lays 250–270 eggs per year!

INQUIRY ACTIVITY

Hands On

Test Matter's Properties

Think about the egg cracking. The egg has many different properties. All matter has different properties based on how it interacts with other matter.

Make a Prediction How can we test the properties of matter?

_____

_____

_____

Carry Out an Investigation

BE CAREFUL Wear safety goggles. Be careful with any sharp or pointy edges on the materials.

1. Hold one end of each object (one at a time) in the ice water for thirty seconds. Did the end you were holding get cold? Record the results in the table on the next page.

2. Pick up each object and gently try to bend it. Did it bend easily? Record the results.

3. Touch the magnet to each of the objects. Did it stick? Record the results.

4. Hold each object under a light. Is it shiny? Record the results.

5. Leave the last column empty for now. You will be revisiting this activity later in the lesson.

Materials

 safety goggles

 acrylic rod

 paper clip

 rubber eraser

 aluminum foil

 copper wire

 wooden toothpicks

 magnet

 plastic bowl

 ice cubes

water

Record Data

Object	Did it get cold?	Could you bend it?	Did the magnet stick to it?	Is it shiny?	What property does it have?
Acrylic Rod					
Paper Clip					
Rubber Eraser					
Aluminum Foil					
Copper Wire					
Wooden Toothpick					

Communicate Information

6. Compare your results with your classmates. Would you expect to have similar results by following the same procedure? Explain.

_____

_____

_____

💬 Talk About It

Did your results support your prediction? Explain.

Matter

Look for these
words as you read:

chemical
  property

conductivity

magnetism

mass

matter

physical
  property

reflectivity

solubility

volume

Matter is anything that has mass and takes up space. The water you drink, the air you breathe, and you are all made up of matter.

All matter is made of tiny particles. **Mass** is a measure of the amount of matter in an object. The more mass an object has, the more particles an object has. Think about holding a golf ball and a table tennis ball. The golf ball is made up of more particles. It has more mass. As you hold the golf ball and table tennis ball, you are also feeling their weight. Weight is how strongly gravity pulls on an object.

The amount of space an object takes up is its **volume**. Volume describes how large or small an object is. A golf ball and table tennis ball have roughly the same volume.

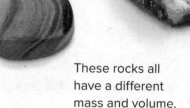

These rocks all have a different mass and volume.

1. Think about an inflated balloon with a small bag of marbles that is half its size. Which one has more volume? Explain your answer.

_____

_____

_____

2. Which one has more mass? Explain your answer.

_____

_____

_____

_____

Physical Properties

A characteristic of matter that can be observed and or measured is known as its **physical property**. These properties can be observed without changing the material. Some physical properties include the following:

Conductivity describes how energy, such as electricity or heat, can move through material. Metals such as iron, silver, and copper are good conductors of heat and electricity.

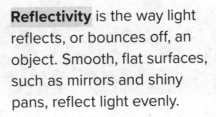

Reflectivity is the way light reflects, or bounces off, an object. Smooth, flat surfaces, such as mirrors and shiny pans, reflect light evenly.

Solubility is the ability of matter to dissolve in a liquid . Think about sugar in a glass of ice tea. The tiny sugar particles disperse evenly throughout the liquid. It might seem like the sugar disappeared, but it is easy to tell it is still there because the tea tastes sweet.

Magnetism is the ability of a material to be attracted to a magnet, without needing to be a magnet itself. Some metals are magnetic.

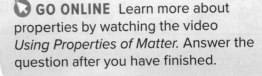

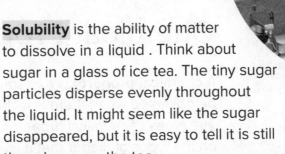

1. How can we use the properties of matter to identify materials?

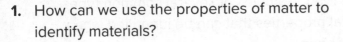

GO ONLINE Learn more about properties by watching the video *Using Properties of Matter*. Answer the question after you have finished.

REVISIT Revist the Page Keeley Science Probe on page 5.
PAGE KEELEY
SCIENCE PROBES

Inspect

Read the passage *Chemical Properties.* Underline text that tells you what makes a property of matter a chemical property.

Find Evidence

Reread the passage with a partner and discuss. Look again at the second page. Highlight text evidence that explains a chemical change that can happen slowly.

Notes

_____

_____

_____

_____

_____

_____

_____

_____

_____

_____

Chemical Properties

A **chemical property** is a characteristic that can only be observed when there is a change in the type of matter. The types of chemical properties of an object depend on the types of matter that it consists of.

Often, we can see, hear, or smell the types of changes caused by chemical properties. You may already have observed examples of several common types of chemical properties that can be identified when matter changes.

Talk About It

Use the lines below to list physical and chemical properties in the photos. Compare lists with your partner.

Notes

When wood burns, it undergoes a change. Being able to burn means that the material is combustible. Some matter, such as food products, can change when they are heated or cooked.

Some materials have a chemical property that causes them to react with air. Some metals will react with air over time and cause it to rust or tarnish. These processes are also called corrosion.

Revisit the activity *Test Matter's Properties*. Use the information from the text to complete the last column of the data table. With a partner, **identify the properties** that you **observed** for each object. Discuss your reasoning.

Cut out the Notebook Foldables tabs given to you by your teacher.
Glue the anchor tabs as shown below. Use what you have learned
about the properties of matter.

Glue your graph here.

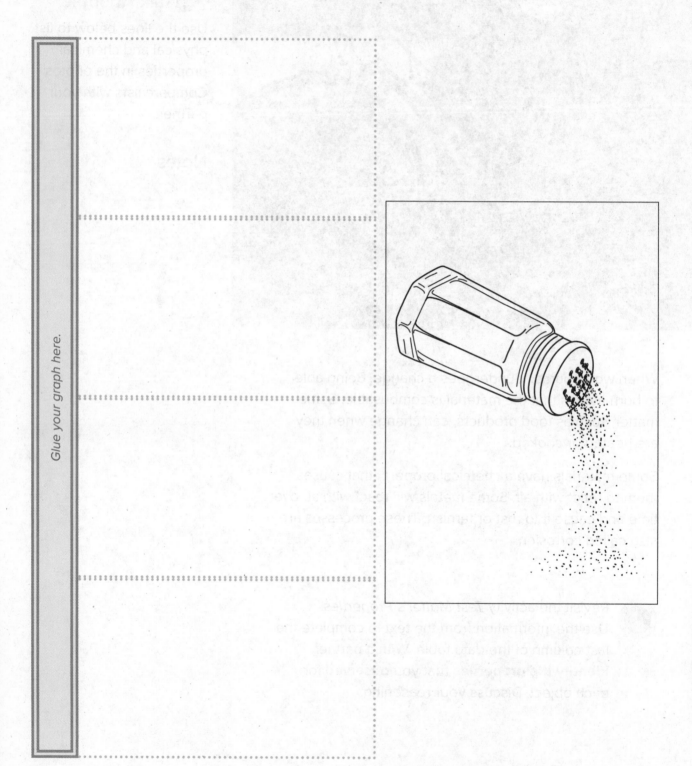

What Does a Materials Scientist Do?

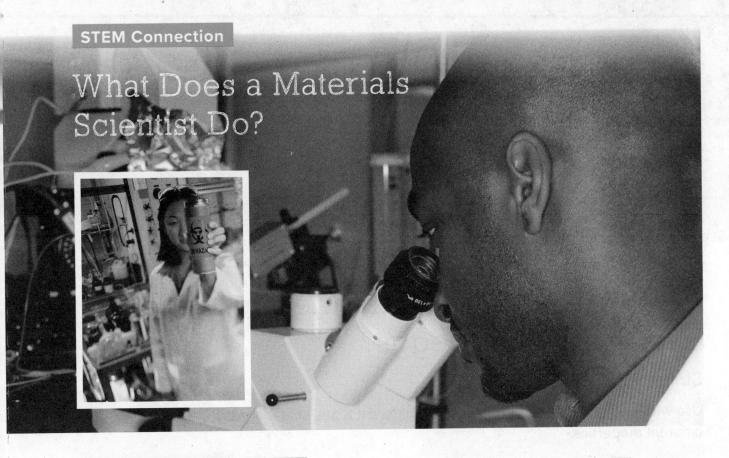

ENVIRONMENTAL Connection

A **materials scientist** tests how different materials can be used together. Materials scientists often try to combine matter into new materials with useful properties. Modern materials scientists combine and change materials based on an understanding of their properties and how matter is put together. They have a responsibility to make sure the materials they test and create are safe for the environment and how they will be used.

It's Your Turn

Think about the role of a materials scientist. As a culinary scientist, what information used by a materials scientist would help you in planning to design the best pancake?

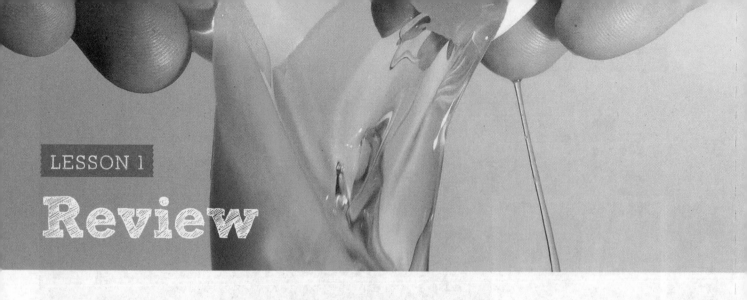

Review

EXPLAIN
THE PHENOMENON

What are the properties of eggs?

Summarize It

Use what you have learned to explain how different types of matter have different properties.

_____

_____

_____

_____

_____

_____

_____

REVISIT
PAGE KEELEY
SCIENCE PROBES

Revisit the Page Keeley Science Probe on page 5. Has your thinking changed? If so, explain how it has changed.

Three-Dimensional Thinking

1. Which property measures the space taken up by an object?

   A. hardness

   B. mass

   C. volume

   D. weight

2. Use information you have obtained to explain how properties of matter can be measured.

   _____

   _____

   _____

   _____

   _____

   _____

   _____

   _____

3. Describe at least three physical properties that can help identify copper.

   _____

   _____

   _____

   _____

   _____

   _____

   _____

   _____

Extend It

Think about a problem you have seen in your community. How could your understanding of the properties of matter help you solve this problem?

Write a proposal to your town council with your solution to the problem.

_____

_____

_____

_____

_____

_____

_____

_____

_____

_____

_____

_____

_____

_____

_____

KEEP PLANNING

STEM Module Project
Engineering Challenge

Now that you have learned how to identify the properties of matter, go to your Module Project to explain how you can use the information as you plan to make the perfect pancake.

Salt and Water

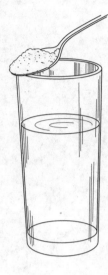

A spoonful of salt has a mass of 10 grams. A cup of water has a mass of 300 grams. What do you predict will be the total mass of the saltwater when the salt is dissolved in the water? Circle the answer that best matches your thinking.

A. *more than 300 grams*

B. *less than 300 grams*

C. *300 grams*

Explain your thinking. What reasoning did you use to make your prediction?

_____

_____

_____

_____

_____

You will revisit the Page Keeley Science Probe later in the lesson.

Mixtures and Solutions

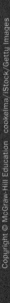

ENCOUNTER
THE PHENOMENON

What is happening to the solid and the liquid?

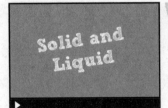

▶ GO ONLINE

Check out *Solid and Liquid* to see the phenomenon in action.

Look at the photo and watch the video of the solid and the liquid. Have you seen something like this before? What questions do you have about the phenomenon?

_____

_____

_____

_____

_____

_____

_____

_____

Did You Know?

The air you breathe is actually a mixture of many different types of gases such as nitrogen, oxygen, and carbon dioxide.

INQUIRY ACTIVITY

Hands On
Solubility Solutions

Think about the phenomenon of the solid being mixed into the liquid. You will investigate whether a solid will dissolve faster in warm water or cold water.

Make a Prediction Will sugar dissolve faster in warm or cold water?

_____

_____

_____

_____

Materials

2 beakers

warm water

cold water

4 spoonfuls of sugar

spoon

stopwatch

Carry Out an Investigation

1. Pour 200 milliliters (mL) of hot tap water into a beaker.

2. Repeat step 1 with cold tap water in a second beaker.

3. Pour 2 spoonfuls of sugar into the hot tap water.

4. Start the stop watch and begin stirring the sugar into the hot tap water with the spoon. Stop the timer when the sugar has dissolved completely. Record the time in the table.

5. Remove the spoon from the beaker. Measure the volume of water in the beaker. Record this data in the table.

6. Repeat steps 3-5 with the cold tap water.

> **GO ONLINE** Watch the video *Measuring Matter* to learn about measuring mass and volume.

DATA

Record Data

	Time to Mix	Volume
Hot Water + Sugar		
Cold Water + Sugar		

Communicate Information

7. Use the data from the table to help you explain whether your results support your prediction.

_____

_____

_____

8. What other variable could you investigate when making mixtures of solids and liquids besides the temperature of a liquid? Using a separate sheet of paper, plan an investigation to explore the cause and effect relationship of the variable on the mixture.

_____

_____

_____

9. **MATH Connection** Your teacher asks you to pour the two mixtures that you made into a container that can hold 1 liter of liquid. Will the container overflow? Show your calculations on a separate piece of paper.

_____

_____

_____

Talk About It

Compare your results from question 7 with a partner. How does this relate to what you learned about the physical property of solubility in Lesson 1?

VOCABULARY

Look for these
words as you read:

colloid

mixture

solution

Types of Mixtures

At first glance, a garden salad and fog seem to have little in common. However, both are mixtures. A **mixture** is a physical combination of two or more substances. A mixture forms when two substances mix, but do not combine chemically. There are many types of mixtures that you probably recognize from things you see every day.

Mixtures that have parts that are not uniformly mixed together are called heterogeneous mixtures. You can see the individual parts of a garden salad. There are no rules in what is mixed, and there can be more of one ingredient or material in some parts than others in heterogeneous mixtures. A suspension is a heterogeneous mixture that looks like it is the same throughout, like muddy water. This example of a suspension can settle out over time, showing the parts of the mixture.

A salad is a heterogeneous mixture.

The appearance of muddy water under a microscope shows that it is a heterogeneous mixture as a suspension. The clay will settle out of the muddy water over time.

A **colloid** is a heterogeneous mixture in which the parts are so small that they do not settle out, like fog. Foam is a colloid that forms when gas bubbles are trapped in a liquid or solid. An example of foam is whipped cream. An aerosol is a colloid where small particles of liquid or solid material are trapped in air. Airborne dust is an example of an aerosol.

Homogeneous mixtures are uniform throughout. A type of homogeneous mixture is a **solution**. Tap water is a homogeneous mixture. It contains dissolved minerals and gases. Sugar water is also an example of a homogeneous mixture. Sugar that is placed in a glass of water dissolves, forming a solution.

A carbonated beverage is a solution of carbon dioxide gas in liquid water under pressure. When the pressure is released, the carbon dioxide gas bubbles out of the solution.

1. List different types of mixtures that you see every day or that you have made. Identify the type of each mixture you list.

Example of a Mixture	Type of Mixture

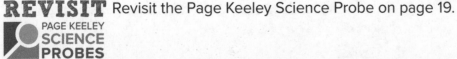
REVISIT Revisit the Page Keeley Science Probe on page 19.

PAGE KEELEY
SCIENCE
PROBES

Simulation

Mixtures in Action

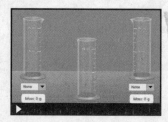

🕹 GO ONLINE

Explore the simulation Mixtures in Action.
Record information about the types of mixtures
you were able to make in the simulation in
the table below.

Make a Prediction When you mix materials together, is the mass of the mixture
the same or different than the sum of the mass of the original materials?

_____

_____

_____

Mass of individual materials: salt—10.9 g, gelatin—7 g, water—5 g,
clay—10 g, pebbles—7.5 g

Materials Mixed	Type of Mixture	Mass of Mixture

Communicate Information

 Use mathematics and computational thinking to explain the relationship of the **mass of the individual materials** and the **mixtures they made**.

_____

_____

_____

_____

WRITING Connection Think about everything you have learned about mixtures. How are mixtures important in your life? Use information from the lesson, give real world examples of mixtures, and research more to support your opinion. Use the graphic organizer below and write your response on a separate sheet of paper.

Main Idea
Detail
Detail
Detail

A Day in the Life of a Chemist

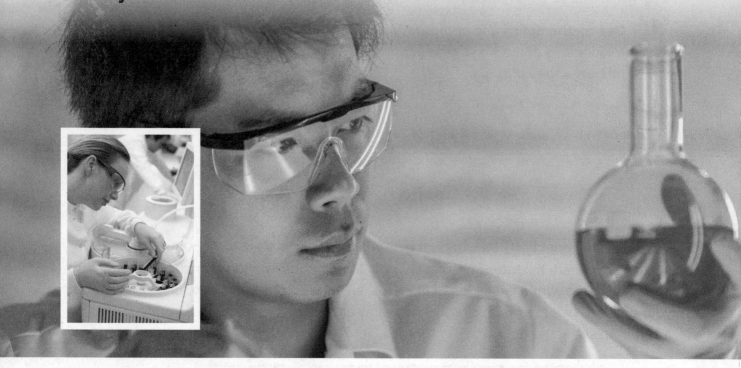

A chemist is a scientist who is an expert in the field of chemistry. Chemistry is the study of matter and its interactions. There are multiple fields that a chemist can focus on. A chemist could work mostly with materials that come from plants and animals, materials that are nonliving or human-made, or with sources of energy.

A day in the life of a chemist depends on what they are studying. They could be in a lab performing research on a new material for a groundbreaking new medicine. Or, they could be exploring an advanced technology. This could involve using a variety of tools that will improve an existing product. Chemists study how matter changes and what causes it to change.

It's Your Turn

How could a chemist separate a mixture that is made? Complete the investigation on the next page to find out.

INQUIRY ACTIVITY

Hands On

Separate Mixtures

You know that a mixture is the physical combination of two or more substances that are blended together. Some mixtures can be easily separated, depending on what they consist of.

Make a Prediction Can a mixture of sand, gravel, and small ball bearings be separated? Why or why not?

_____

_____

_____

_____

Plan an Investigation

BE CAREFUL Wear safety goggles to protect your eyes.

Look at the materials. Plan an investigation to separate a mixture of sand, gravel, and small ball bearings.

1. _____

2. _____

3. _____

4. _____

5. _____

💬 Talk About It

Discuss your results with a partner or another group. Do your results support your prediction?

Copyright © McGraw-Hill Education (1 2 7)Ken Cavanagh/McGraw-Hill Education, (4)3dalia/iStock/Getty Images, (6)Janette Beckman/McGraw-Hill Education, (others)Jacques Cornell/McGraw-Hill Education

Materials

 safety goggles

 1 cup of sand

 1 cup of gravel

 1/8 cup of small ball bearings

 2 bowls

 spoon

 sieve

 magnet

Review

EXPLAIN
THE PHENOMENON

What is happening to the solid and the liquid?

Summarize It

Use what you have learned about mixtures and solutions to explain what is happening to the solid and the liquid.

_____

_____

_____

_____

_____

_____

_____

REVISIT
PAGE KEELEY
SCIENCE PROBES

Revisit the Page Keeley Science Probe on page 19. Has your thinking changed? If so, explain how it has changed.

Three-Dimensional Thinking

1. Which mixture is most likely a solution?

    A. muddy water

    B. cranberry juice

    C. potting soil

    D. milk

2. How are mixtures formed and separated?

_____

_____

_____

_____

_____

_____

_____

_____

_____

_____

_____

_____

_____

_____

_____

_____

_____

_____

Extend It

Think like a chemist. You have just discovered a new medicine while performing research in the lab that will cure the flu with a simple pill. What would you do next? Write a speech that you could deliver at the next conference or gathering of doctors you attend stating the impact this type of medicine would have on the world.

_____

_____

_____

_____

_____

_____

_____

_____

_____

_____

_____

_____

_____

KEEP PLANNING

STEM Module Project
Engineering Challenge

Now that you have learned about mixtures and solutions, go to your Module Project to explain how you can use the information as you plan to make the perfect pancake.

Chemical Change

Frying an egg	Tearing up paper	Burning wood
A nail rusting	Grilling a hamburger	Dissolving salt in water
Exploding fireworks	Melting butter	Baking a cake
Rotting banana	Mixing baking soda and vinegar	Evaporating water
Lighting a match	Crushing a sugar cube	Milk going sour

Changes in matter can be chemical or physical. Put an X in any of the boxes that are examples of chemical changes.

Explain your thinking. How did you decide if something is a chemical change?

_____

_____

_____

_____

You will revisit the Page Keeley Science Probe later in the lesson.

Physical and Chemical Changes

What is causing the banana to change?

Browning Bananas

▶ GO ONLINE

Check out *Browning Bananas* to see the phenomenon in action.

Look at the photos and watch the video of the banana as it changes over time. What questions do you have about the phenomenon? Record or illustrate your thoughts below.

Did You Know?

Bananas grow in tropical climates, in places like Florida and Hawaii in the United States, as well as South America, Central America, and parts of Africa.

INQUIRY ACTIVITY

Hands On

Conservation of Mass

Think about how matter changes, such as the browning bananas. Investigate if the mass of matter changes when it appears to change.

Make a Prediction Is mass conserved when matter combines with other matter?

_____

_____

_____

_____

_____

_____

Materials

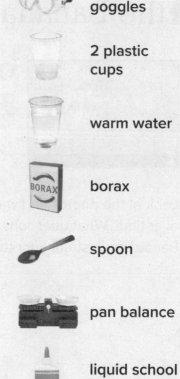

safety goggles

2 plastic cups

warm water

borax

spoon

pan balance

liquid school glue

Carry Out an Investigation

BE CAREFUL Wear safety goggles during the investigation.

1. Fill one cup less than halfway with water. Put an equal amount of liquid school glue into the second cup.

2. Measure the mass of both cups separately and together. Record the mass in the data table on the next page.

3. Pour the water into the glue and mix them with a spoon.

4. Your teacher will add a spoonful of borax solution (about 5 grams) to your cup. Stir well with a spoon and observe.

5. Place both the empty cup and the cup with the mixture on the pan balance together. Record your result in the last column of the table.

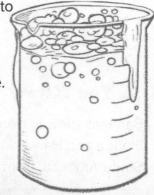

Record Data

Mass of Cup with Water	Mass of Cup with Glue	Mass of Cups before Reaction (including borax solution)	Mass of Cups after Reaction

Communicate Information

6. What did you observe when materials from the two cups were mixed?

_____

_____

_____

_____

💬 Talk About It

Compare your results with a partner. How does this relate to what you learned about mixtures and solutions in Lesson 2?

INQUIRY ACTIVITY

7. **MATH ▶ Connection** Make a bar graph of the mass of the materials before and after the reaction based on the results of the investigation.

Did the matter after the reaction in this activity result in a new substance? **Plan and conduct an investigation** about how you could find out.

_____

_____

_____

_____

_____

_____

_____

MAKE YOUR CLAIM

How can you identify physical and chemical changes?

Make your claim. Use your investigation.

CLAIM

Chemical changes _____, while physical changes _____.

Cite evidence from the activity.

EVIDENCE

The investigation showed that _____.

Discuss your reasoning as a class. Tell about your discussion.

REASONING

The evidence supports the claim because _____.

You will revisit your claim to add more evidence later in this lesson.

Look for these
words as you read:

**chemical
change**

**conservation of
mass**

**physical
change**

Changes in Matter

Think about the ways the banana
was changing. Matter can be
changed in many ways. A
physical change begins and ends
with the same kind of matter. A
chemical change—also called a chemical reaction—is a change
that produces new matter with different properties from the
original matter. The law of **conservation of mass** states that
matter is neither created nor destroyed during a physical
change or chemical reaction. For example, when you mix
baking soda with vinegar, particles in the baking soda and
vinegar link up in new ways. During the chemical change,
bubbles form and a solid is left behind. The new substances
formed have different properties than the starting materials.

GO ONLINE Watch the video
Identifying Chemical Changes
to learn more about how to
recognize a chemical change.

The properties
of a piece of paper
do not change if it is
flat or folded into
a different shape.

After baking
soda and vinegar
react, water and
a type of salt remain,
and carbon dioxide
bubbles are
released.

FOLDABLES®

Cut out the Notebook Foldables® tabs given to you by your teacher. Glue the anchor tabs as shown below. Use what you have learned to describe chemical changes in matter.

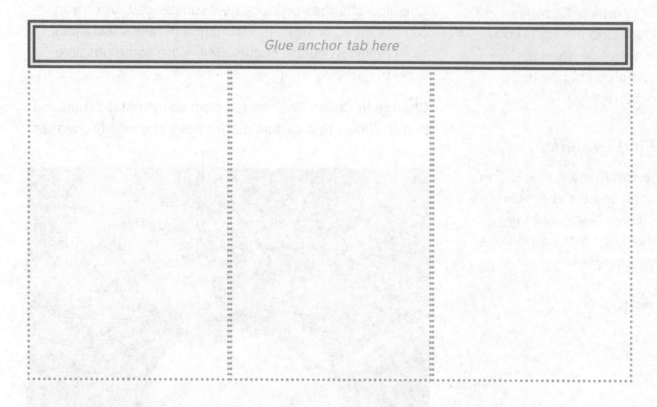

Glue anchor tab here

WRITING Connection Use what you learned to write a paragraph about the physical and chemical changes that you see every day on a separate sheet of paper.

▶ GO ONLINE Watch the video *Property Changes* to learn more about chemical and physical change.

 **REVISIT PAGE KEELEY SCIENCE PROBES** Revisit the Page Keeley Science Probe on page 33.

Inspect

Read the passage *Signs of Chemical Change.* Underline the signs you may notice when a chemical change has occurred.

Find Evidence

Reread Why is soap scum considered a chemical change? Highlight the evidence that supports your answer.

Notes

_____

_____

_____

_____

_____

_____

_____

_____

_____

_____

Signs of Chemical Change

Chemical changes produce new substances. Often you can see, hear, or smell the formation of new substances as a chemical change occurs. Below are some possible signs of chemical change.

Change in Color The change from shiny metal to rust and tarnish shows that certain metals have chemically changed.

Change in Odor Have you ever toasted marshmallows over a campfire? An uncooked marshmallow has little odor. While your marshmallow is toasting, it gives off a pleasant smell. This change in odor is evidence of a chemical change.

Temperature Change Many reactions cause matter to become warm or cold. Sometimes they also give off light, like when you burn wood. However, temperature change can also be part of a physical change, like water freezing.

Formation of a Gas Bubbles or fizzing can indicate the release of a gas. For example, dropping antacid tablets into water will release bubbles that are the result of chemical change. Bubbles in soda are not a result of a chemical change, however.

Formation of a Solid Chemical reactions of some solutions can form a solid. One example is soap scum. Soap scum forms when dissolved soap reacts with tiny particles or minerals dissolved in tap water.

Describe the cause and effect of one of the examples of a chemical change that you read about.

_____

_____

_____

_____

_____

_____

_____

Copyright © McGraw-Hill Education   Robert Neumann/Shutterstock

COLLECT EVIDENCE

Add evidence to your claim on page 39 about how you can identify physical and chemical changes.

Make Connections
💬 Talk About It

Why is a color change such as rust on a shiny metal considered a chemical change while painting a wooden fence is not?

Notes

_____

_____

_____

_____

_____

_____

_____

_____

_____

_____

_____

_____

_____

_____

_____

_____

_____

_____

How Could You Become a Chemist?

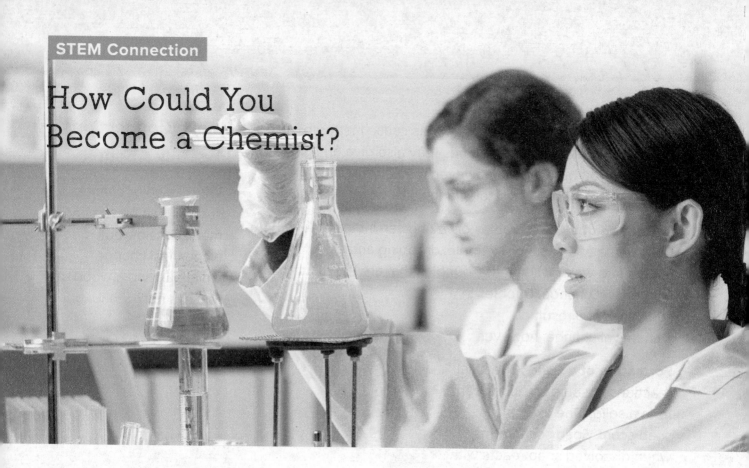

Becoming a **chemist** is a noble career goal! Chemists can work in a variety of fields. You can start to take courses in high school to get an introduction to chemistry and higher-level math. This can help you figure out if you want to pursue a career as a chemist.

If you want to become a chemist, you will take college courses in science and math. You will also have the opportunity to get hands-on experience working with chemists in the field or helping with research in the lab. This will help you learn how to work with a team to solve problems as a chemist.

It's Your Turn

Some chemists specialize in food science. How could a chemist help design the perfect pancake?

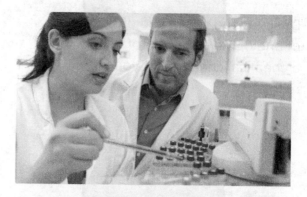

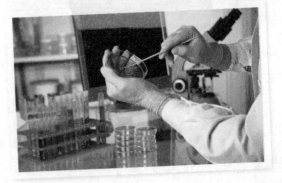

Antoine Lavoisier is considered the father of modern chemistry. His biggest accomplishment came from documenting very detailed experiments that he completed. Lavoisier believed in exact measurements. He discovered that matter is maintained during an experiment, including chemical reactions. You know this as the law of conservation of mass.

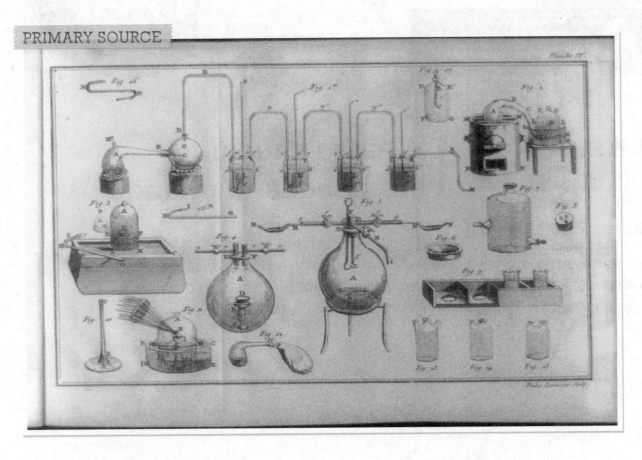

How does the setup of the experiment in the photo allow for conservation of mass to be observed?

Review

EXPLAIN
THE PHENOMENON

| What is causing the banana to change?

Summarize It

Use what you have learned to explain what you know about physical and chemical changes. Use the space below to write a summary or draw a diagram of what can happen when materials are mixed.

REVISIT Revisit the Page Keeley Science Probe on page 33. Has your thinking changed? If so, explain how it has changed.

PAGE KEELEY
SCIENCE
PROBES

Three-Dimensional Thinking

Think about a scenario for an experiment. You combine 500 g of one material and 200 g of another in a closed container. A chemical reaction occurs. What can you say about the mass of the materials after they combine and go through the reaction? Choose a simple mathematical equation to support your answer.

A. 500 g − 200 g = 700 g

B. 500 g + 200 g = 700 g

C. 700 g − 500 g = 200 g

D. 500 g × 200 g = 700 g

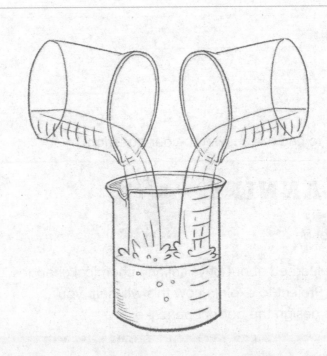

Extend It

⚙ ENGINEERING Connection Use what you have learned about conservation of matter during a chemical and physical change to design a prototype for a device that prepares food without any waste. Draw a diagram of the device with an explanation of how it can prepare food without wasting anything in the process.

OPEN INQUIRY

What question do you still have about chemical changes in matter?

_____

_____

_____

Plan an investigation to find the answer to your question.

KEEP PLANNING

STEM Module Project
Engineering Challenge

Now that you have learned about physical and chemical changes, go to your Module Project to explain how this will help you understand how to design the perfect pancake.

LESSON 4 LAUNCH

Particles in Matter

Four friends were talking about the particles that make up matter and give matter its properties. They each had different ideas. This is what they said:

Joyce: *I think you can't see the particles that make up solids, liquids, and gases. They are too small to see.*

Harold: *I think you can see the particles that make up solids, liquids, and gases.*

Royce: *I think you can see the particles that make up solids and liquids, but you can't see the particles that make up gases.*

Benito: *I think you can see the particles that make up solids, but you can't see the particles that make up liquids and gases.*

Who do you agree with most? _____

Explain why you agree.

_____

_____

_____

_____

You will revisit the Page Keeley Science Probe later in the lesson.

Solids, Liquids, and Gases

ENCOUNTER
THE PHENOMENON

What are the different forms in which matter can appear?

GO ONLINE

Check out *Ice Melting* to see the phenomenon in action.

Look at the photo and watch the video. What questions do you have about the phenomenon? Record or illustrate your thoughts below.

Did You Know?

There is a fourth state of matter called plasma. The Sun and all the stars in the universe are made up of plasma.

INQUIRY ACTIVITY

Hands On

Observe Matter

Think about the phenomenon of the melting ice. You know that the ice and water are made of the same material, but they appear in different forms.

Make a Prediction Can we easily change the shape of different types of matter?

_____

_____

_____

_____

Carry Out an Investigation

Station 1

1. Draw air into the syringe and cover the opposite end with your finger.

2. Push on the plunger.

3. Record your observations in the box below.

Materials

 syringe

 sponge

 number cube

 modeling clay

 large beaker

 water

 graduated cylinder

Station 2

4. Squeeze the sponge. Observe what happens to its shape. Record your observations in the box below.

5. Squeeze the number cube between your fingers. Observe what happens to its shape. Record your observations.

6. Squeeze the modeling clay. Observe what happens to its shape. Record your observations.

INQUIRY ACTIVITY

7. Fill the beaker halfway with water.

8. Pour some of the water from the beaker into the graduated cylinder. Record your observations in the box below.

Communicate Information

9. Did your results support your prediction? Explain how your prediction was or was not supported by what you observed.

_____

_____

_____

_____

_____

MAKE YOUR CLAIM

How do the three states of matter change shape?

Make your claim. Use your investigation.

CLAIM
Solids _____. Liquids _____. Gas _____.

Cite evidence from the activity.

EVIDENCE
The investigation showed that _____.

Discuss your reasoning as a class. Tell about your discussion.

REASONING
The evidence supports the claim because _____.

You will revisit your claim to add more evidence later in this lesson.

VOCABULARY

Look for these words as you read:

gas

liquid

solid

State is another physical property of matter. Solids, liquids, and gases are common forms that matter can take. Each state has specific characteristics.

GO ONLINE Watch the video *States of Matter* to learn more about matter.

A **solid** has a definite shape and takes up a definite amount of space. A solid stays in its definite shape with a definite volume unless it is changed by an outside force. The particles in a solid are tightly packed together and vibrate in place. They are often packed in a regular pattern.

A **liquid** has a definite volume, but it does not have a definite shape. It can be poured from one container to another. The liquid fills the shape it is poured into from the bottom up. The particles in a liquid are usually less tightly packed than those in a solid and can move and slide past one another. One example in which this is not true is water. Water is actually more dense than ice!

Books have a definite shape. No matter what type of container you put them in they will still keep that shape.

The liquid being poured from this bottle is able to flow because it does not have a definite shape.

Because the basketball is a sphere, the air inside of it will be sphere-shaped too.

Gases have no definite shape or volume. The particles in a gas are much farther apart than particles in solids or liquids. They can move around each other very easily. Gases spread out and completely fill a closed container. If you make the container bigger, the same amount of gas will expand to fill it.

INQUIRY ACTIVITY

Simulation

Particles in Matter

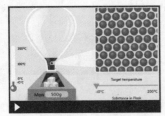

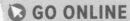
GO ONLINE

Explore the simulation *Particles in Matter*.
Record data from the simulation in
the table below.

Make a Prediction How does temperature affect the state and mass of
different types of matter?

_____

_____

_____

Type of Matter	Temperature	State of Matter	Mass
Iodine	−10° C		
	200° C		
Ethanol	−10° C		
	200° C		
Olive Oil	−10° C		
	200° C		

1. Explain the movement of the particles as you add energy to
   each substance.

   _____

   _____

2. What happens to the mass of the materials in the simulation
   regardless of whether heat is added or removed?

   _____

   _____

Changing States of Matter

The average movement of particles in an object is determined by the amount of energy in the object. Temperature is a measurement of this movement. When energy is added, the particles move faster. When energy is lost, the particles move more slowly. When enough energy is gained or lost, there is a change of state.

Adding Energy When energy is added to a solid, the particles start to move more quickly. When the particles move quickly enough that they slide past each other, the solid becomes a liquid by melting. If even more energy is added to this liquid, the particles' speed continues to increase and they move away from each other. As the particles spread out enough, liquid evaporates, becoming a gas.

Removing Energy If a gas loses energy, its particles slow down and move closer together. They start to slide past each other again. A liquid forms through a process called condensation. If the liquid loses enough energy, freezing occurs and a solid forms.

Label a Diagram Use information that you read to label the states of matter in the diagram above. Label the process of how each state of matter changes from one to the other.

COLLECT EVIDENCE

Add evidence to your claim on page 55. Use what you have learned about the changing states of matter to add evidence and reasoning to your claim.

REVISIT Revisit the Page Keeley Science Probe on page 49.

PAGE KEELEY
SCIENCE
PROBES

Model Matter

You have learned about the three main states of matter and how the organization of their particles affects how they behave.

 Choose an object for each of the three states of matter. Draw each object. Use unit cubes to **develop and use a model** to show the scale of the volume and number of particles in the object and how the particles in each object are organized. Add this information to your drawings. Below each model, describe how the arrangement of the particles determines the properties of each of the objects.

Solid	Liquid	Gas

A Day in the Life of a Pharmacy Technician

Pharmacy technicians work in hospitals and pharmacies. They work closely with pharmacists and people in the health industry. Some technicians are responsible for inputting prescription orders given over the phone or in person. They take orders from both patients and health care providers. Pharmacy technicians are also responsible for counting pills, mixing medicines, and labeling prescriptions.

Pharmacy technicians need to have good communication skills as they interact with patients on a regular basis. They relay information from the pharmacist to patients. They give out prescription medication and medical devices to patients. They explain how to use the prescription, what it is for, and how often to take it. They also explain what the patient can expect when taking a prescription.

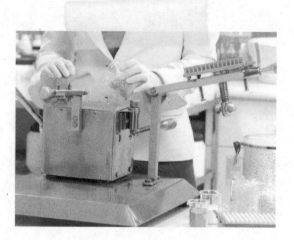

It's Your Turn

What types of information does a pharmacy technician need to know about matter?

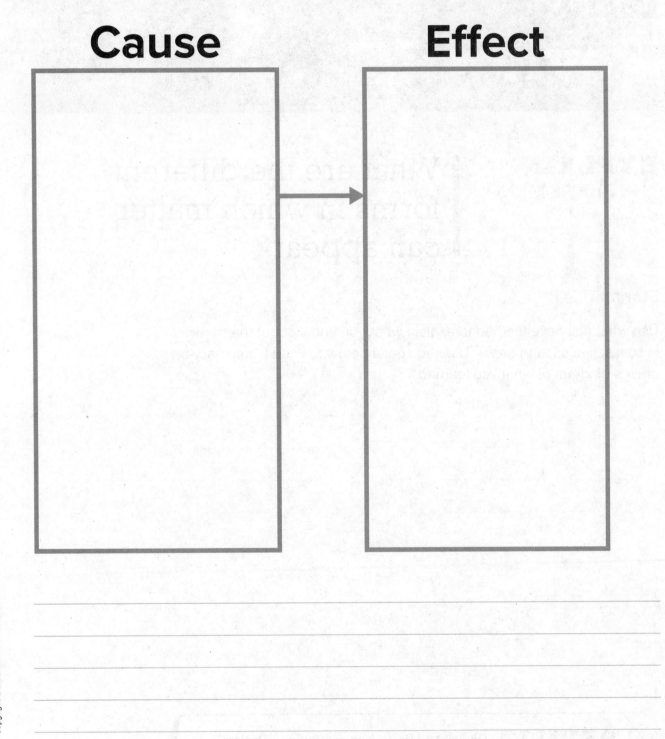

Review

EXPLAIN
THE PHENOMENON

What are the different forms in which matter can appear?

Summarize It

Use what you have learned to explain what you know about the particles in solids, liquids, and gases. Use the space below to write a summary or draw a diagram of what you learned.

REVISIT

PAGE KEELEY SCIENCE PROBES

Revisit the Page Keeley Science Probe on page 49. Has your thinking changed? If so, explain how it has changed.

Three-Dimensional Thinking

1. How does matter change from one state to another?
   Circle all that apply.

   A. adding energy

   B. removing energy

   C. adding mass

   D. removing volume

2. Liquid has _____. Circle all that apply.

   A. definite volume

   B. definite shape

   C. no definite volume

   D. no definite shape

3. Use evidence to support the argument that particles in water change when heat energy is added.

_____

_____

_____

_____

_____

_____

_____

_____

_____

_____

Extend It

A type of matter called plasma is the fourth state of matter. It is mostly found in stars and other planets in space. Conduct a short research project on plasma. Use multimedia to organize your research and present it to the class.

_____

_____

_____

_____

_____

_____

_____

_____

_____

_____

_____

_____

_____

_____

_____

KEEP PLANNING

STEM Module Project
Engineering Challenge

Now that you have learned about how the states of matter behave based on their structure, move on to your Module Project to explain how the information will affect your pancake recipe.

Design the Perfect Pancake

You are going to use the skills of a culinary scientist to develop the "perfect" pancake. You will identify the criteria and the different materials needed to make the best pancake. Use what you have learned throughout the module to design and test different ingredients to make the best pancake.

Planning after Lesson 1

Apply what you have learned about the properties of materials to your project planning.

What would the perfect pancake look like to you? How does knowing about the properties of the materials affect how well you could cook a pancake?

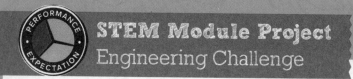
Planning after Lesson 2

Apply what you have learned about mixtures and solutions to your project planning.

What factors should be considered when mixing ingredients for your module project?

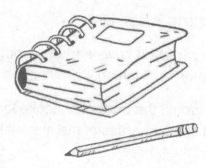

Planning after Lesson 3

Apply what you have learned about how matter changes to continue your project planning.

Explain how physical and chemical changes will affect the mixture of materials in your pancake batter.

Planning after Lesson 4

Apply what you have learned about solids, liquids, and gases to your project planning.

How will your understanding of the state of matter affect your module project?

Research the Problem

Research ideas for materials that could be used in your project by going online to teacher-approved websites, by interviewing a chef, or by finding cookbooks from your local library.

Source	Information to Use in My Project

Keep Planning

Plan your recipe for the perfect pancake. Write your ideas on a separate piece of paper. Select the best one to test.

Design the Perfect Pancake

Look back at the planning you did after each lesson. Use that information and the rest of the Engineering Design Process to complete your final module project.

The Engineering Design Process

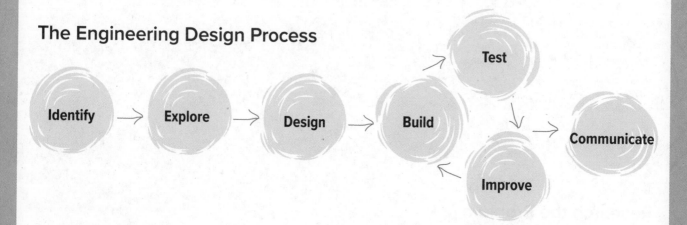

Build Your Model

1. Use your project planning. Define what you think the perfect pancake should be like below.

2. Write clear steps to test your model.

3. Define the materials to make and test your design. List the materials in the space to the right.

4. Discuss the criteria with the class. Your pancake should pass all the criteria.

5. Record the improvements made to the design after each trial.

Materials

_____

_____

_____

_____

_____

_____

_____

_____

Procedure

_____

_____

_____

_____

_____

_____

_____

Test Your Model

Make and test your design. Record your observations and results.
Use a data table if you need to.

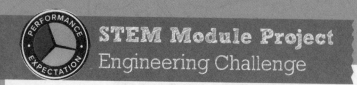
Communicate Your Results

Share the plan for your pancake and your results with another group. Compare how well each of your group's procedure was able to fairly test your plan for the perfect pancake. Communicate your findings below.

_____

_____

_____

_____

_____

_____

_____

_____

_____

_____

_____

MATH Connection You are hired as a chef to prepare breakfast for a large group. You know that the cost of making eight pancakes is $2.55. How much would it cost to make two hundred pancakes?

_____

_____

_____

_____

_____

MODULE WRAP-UP

REVISIT
THE PHENOMENON

Using what you learned in this module, explain how understanding the properties of matter can help you develop the perfect pancake.

Revisit your project if you need to gather more evidence.

How have your ideas changed?

_____

_____

Science Glossary

A

abiotic factor a nonliving part of an ecosystem

acid rain harmful rain caused by the burning of fossil fuels

air mass a large region of air that has a similar temperature and humidity

algae bloom a sometimes harmful rapid increase in the amount of algae found in water

apparent motion when a star or other object in the sky seems to move even though it is Earth that is moving

atmosphere the gases that surround Earth

B

bacteria a type of single cell organism

biosphere the part of Earth in which living things exist and interact

biotic factor a living thing in an ecosystem, such as a plant, an animal, or a bacterium

C

chemical change a change that produces new matter with different properties from the original matter

chemical property a characteristic that can only be observed when the type of matter changes

climate the average weather pattern of a region over time

colloid a type of mixture in which the particles of one material are scattered through another without settling out

condensation the process through which a gas changes into a liquid

conductivity ability for energy, such as electricity and heat, to move through a material

conservation the act of saving, protecting, or using resources wisely

conservation of mass a physical law that states that matter is neither created nor destroyed during a physical or chemical change

constellation any of the patterns of stars that can be seen in the night sky from here on Earth

consumer an organism that cannot make its own food

D

decomposer an organism that breaks down dead plant and animal material

deforestation the removal of trees from a large area

deposition the dropping off of eroded soil and bits of rock

E

endangered when a species is in danger of becoming extinct

energy the ability to do work or change something

energy flow the movement of energy from one organism to another in a food chain or food web

erosion the process of weathered rock moving from one place to another

evaporation a process through which a liquid changes into a gas

extinct when a species has died out completely

F

floodplain land near a body of water that is likely to flood

food chain the path that energy and nutrients follow among living things in an ecosystem

food web the overlapping food chains in an ecosystem

fungi plant-like organisms that get energy from other organisms which may be living or dead

G

galaxy a collection of billions of stars, dust and gas that is held together by gravity

gas a state of matter that does not have its own shape or definite volume

geosphere the layers of solid and molten rock, dirt, and soil on Earth

glacier a large sheet of ice that moves slowly across the land

gravity the force of attraction between any two objects due to their mass

groundwater water stored in the cracks and spaces between particles of soil and underground rocks

H

habitat a place where plants and animals live

hot spot an area where molten rock from within the mantle rises close to Earth's surface

hydrosphere Earth's water, whether found on land or in oceans, including the freshwater found underground and in glaciers, lakes, and rivers

I

ice caps a covering of ice over a large area such as in the polar regions

invasive species an organism that is introduced to a new ecosystem and causes harm

L

landslide the sudden movement of rocks and soil down a slope

light year the distance light travels in a year

liquids a state of matter that has a definite volume but no definite shape

M

magnetism the ability of a material to be attracted to a magnet without needing to be a magnet themselves

mass the amount of material in an object

matter anything that has mass and takes up space

meteor a chunk of rock from space that travels through Earth's atmosphere

meteorite A meteor that strikes Earth's surface

minerals solid, nonliving substances found in nature

mixture a physical combination of two or more substances that are blended together without forming new substances

molten rock very hot melted rock found in Earth's mantle

moon phases the apparent shapes of the Moon in the sky

N

nitrogen cycle the continuous circulation of nitrogen from air to soil to organisms and back to air or soil

O

orbit the path an object takes as it travels around another object

oxygen-carbon cycle the continuous exchange of carbon dioxide and oxygen among living things

P

phloem the tissue through which food from the leaves moves throughout the rest of a plant

physical change a change of matter in size, shape, or state that does not change the type of matter

physical property a characteristic of matter that can be observed and or measured

planet a large, round object in space that orbits a star

precipitation water that falls from clouds to the ground in the form of rain, sleet, hail, or snow

predator an animal that hunts other animals for food

prey animals that are eaten by other animals

producer an organism that uses energy from the Sun to make its own food

R

reflectivity the way light bounces off an object

reservoir an artificial lake built for storage of water

revolution one complete trip around an object in a circular or nearly circular path

rotation a complete spin on an axis

runoff excess water that flows over Earth's surface from a storm or flood

S

solid a state of matter that has a definite shape and volume

solubility the maximum amount of a substance that can be dissolved by another substance

solution a mixture of substances that are blended so completely that the mixture looks the same everywhere

star an object in space that produces its own energy, including heat and light

stomata pores in the bottom of leaves that open and close to let in air or give off water vapor

storage the process of water being stored on Earth's surface in the ground or as a water feature

T

tides the regular rise and fall of the water level along a shoreline

transpiration the release of water vapor through the stomata of a plant

V

volcano an opening in Earth's surface where melted rock or gases are forced out

volume a measure of how much space an object takes up

W

water cycle the continuous movement of water between Earth's surface and the air, changing from liquid into gas into liquid

weather the condition of the atmosphere at a given place and time

X

xylem the plant tissue through which water and minerals move up from the roots

Index

T

V

Dinah Zike's
Visual
Kinesthetic
Vocabulary ®

✂ cut on all dashed lines

▢ fold on all solid lines

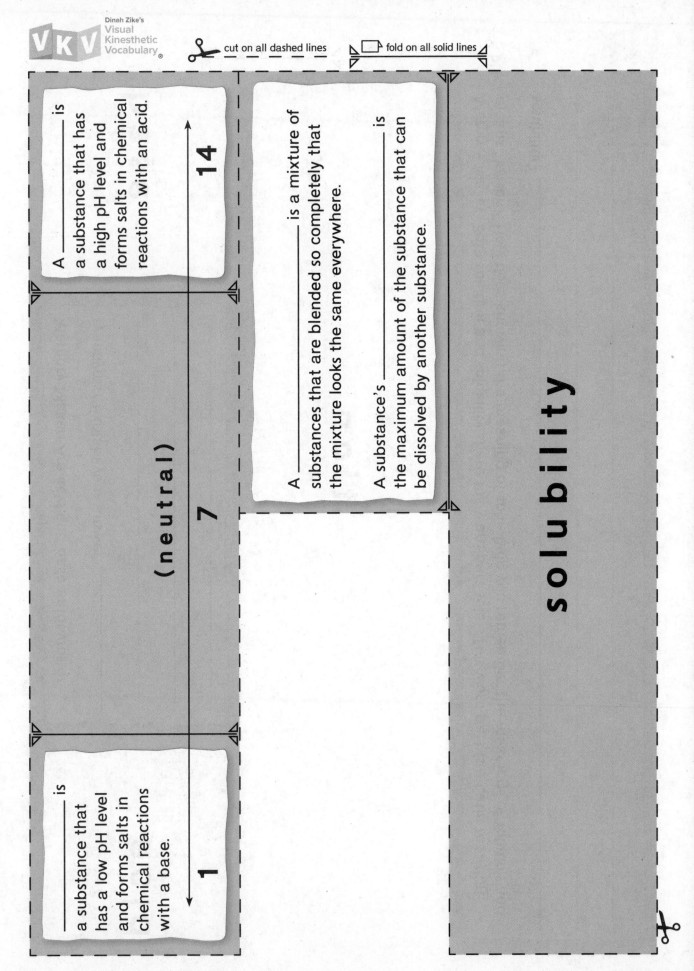

A ___ is a substance that has a high pH level and forms salts in chemical reactions with an acid.

14

(neutral)

7

A ___ is a mixture of substances that are blended so completely that the mixture looks the same everywhere.

A substance's ___ is the maximum amount of the substance that can be dissolved by another substance.

A ___ is a substance that has a low pH level and forms salts in chemical reactions with a base.

1

solubility

Dinah Zike's
VKV
Visual
Kinesthetic
Vocabulary®

✂ cut on all dashed lines   fold on all solid lines

base

tion

acid

Memory Maker: Are **acid** and **base** antonyms or synonyms? Explain your answer.

Memory Maker: Both **solution** and **solubility** share the word part **solu-**. This word part is a Latin root that means "loosen." How does knowing the meaning of **solu-** help you remember the meanings of **solution** and **solubility**?